Judith Oringer studied piano at the Manhattan School of Music and the High School of Music & Art. She has published numerous interviews with artists and writes about music, literature, politics, and women. Currently a French interpreter for the U.S. State Department, she resides in New York City.

Passion for the Piano

Passion for the Piano

Judith Oringer

foreword by André Watts

JEREMY P. TARCHER, INC.
Los Angeles
Distributed by Houghton Mifflin Company
Boston

Library of Congress Cataloging in Publication Data

Oringer, Judith
Passion for the piano
1. Piano. I. Title.
ML650.074 1983 786.1 83-4862
ISBN 0-87477-288-5
ISBN 0-87477-280-X (pbk.)

Jeremy P. Tarcher, Inc.
9110 Sunset Boulevard
Los Angeles, California 90069

Design by Tanya Maiboroda

MANUFACTURED IN THE UNITED STATES OF AMERICA

10 9 8 7 6 5 4 3 2 1

First Edition

CONTENTS

To my mother, Estelle Parnas Oringer, a passionate and outstanding pianist if there ever was one. Words can't express how much your unending love and support of me means, particularly while I was writing this book. Thank you for being such an inspiration to me and to others with your joyful spirit, your great musical gift, your brilliance, and your profound lovingness.

This book is also dedicated to everyone with a passion for the piano. Long may it live!

Acknowledgments

So many people with a passion for the piano have made a contribution to this book in their own ways. I thank each and every one of them: pianists, their managers and representatives, teachers, tuners, librarians, museum archivists, photographers, and people whose names I will never know. You know who you are.

Special thanks to John Steinway, of Steinway & Sons, who opened up those grand doors; Bernard Groger, who believed in the project from the start; Robbie Konikoff of Moog Music, for sending so many fine musicians my way; Jack Romann of Baldwin, helpful and delightful at every step of the way; and Constance Keene, head of the Piano Department at the Manhattan School of Music, for her marvelous encouragement and pianistic wisdom. Several photo researchers enriched this book: Rebecca Hirsch, "our girl" in Washington, who was always so in tune; Alan Foreman, for his clarity and direction; Yvonne Freund, for her great research knowledge and care; and Kristin Murphy, for her inspiration. Joel Honig added his meticulous scholarly attention and sense of humor. Mark Freedman opened the gates of the new electronic realm in music for me, as did Craig Hazen and George Gelish. Gerry Nordgren shared his jazz passion.

My aunt, Sara Marcus, was a great support for me. So was knowing of my father's love and appreciation of me. Audrey Hagemaier understood my vision and kept me, playfully, on track. Many of my friends contributed enormously in keeping me together, body and spirit, during the writing of this book, particularly: Wade Hampton, Bob Larzelere, Sheila Mayer, Harvey Fish, Frenie Sewell, Kathy Erlandson, and my agent, Caroline Latham.

The great teachers in my life—those who taught me in spirit, as well as those who taught me in person—counted, as always: Sybil Mandel, of the High School of Music & Art in New York City; the Manhattan School of Music; my mother; the University of California at Berkeley, and the city of Berkeley; Paris, France; Simone de Beauvoir; David Horowitz and Peter Collier of the old *Ramparts*; Anaïs Nin; Werner Erhard; Joan Holmes and The Hunger Project; Janet Tucker; Tom Jackson; Leonard Bernstein; and of course, Artur Rubinstein. Con brio!

Special thanks to my editor, Janice Gallagher, for her foresight, her consummate editorial skills, and for always keeping a lively beat. To Robin Raphaelian, for her seamless art and commitment. And to Jeremy Tarcher, a creative, adventurous publisher.

Acknowledgments

Foreword

The greatest passion in my life is the piano. It is a quiet passion, a smolderingly constant passion, passion that simply *is* without any flag waving, trumpets, or fanfares. Judith Oringer has transposed this passion from the keyboard to the printed page. Not only does she sense the growing fascination with the piano that is sweeping the country, but she even takes note of the interesting new acoustical developments in the instrument itself and what those changes will mean to pianists.

This, then, is the perfect moment for *Passion for the Piano.* This book is an up-to-date companion to the accepted academic classics about pianos and pianists, and it presages a new era. Its author gives dimension, breadth, and vision to the passion for the piano—and of the pianist—in the 1980s.

I had the uncanny sensation that Judith Oringer had been peering over my shoulder throughout my experience as a pianist. So many aspects of my piano life come alive in this book: the joys and realities of performing, the mysteries of piano tuning, the fascination of piano manufacturing, the pleasures of learning—and teaching—the piano, the exciting extensions of the piano into every corner of modern life—the arts, politics, film, literature, graphics, history, social life, and intrigue. What a magnificent role the piano plays!

I'm tickled every time I read about how Chopin named his famous "Minute Waltz"—after watching his lover Georges Sand's dog running around in circles trying to chase its tail. How piano tuners ply their trade in the most unlikely places—barns, lofts, ships, even the Paris métro—and are subject to all sorts of propositions, not all of them musical! And how there are more and more "crossover" pianists, such as jazz pianist Chick Corea, who is now adding Mozart to his repertoire, and Keith Jarrett, who is playing Bartók piano concertos. It's even surprising to find out where the piano bars, concert halls, and music shops are found, everywhere from Atlanta to Seattle, as well as other fascinating facts a good source book such as this one offers. I also learned a few intriguing bits of piano lore myself, ranging from the humorous to the tragically absurd. Did you know that a Bösendorfer piano was thrown off the *Queen Elizabeth II* into the ocean during the Falkland Islands conflict to make room for helicopters?

In *Passion for the Piano* people can read about their own passion for the instrument and discover all the varieties of passion that exist under the sun for others. They may unearth new aspects of their passion that are buried deep within and have not yet been brought to the fore. *Passion for the Piano* will hook everyone from the amateur who practices five minutes a week to the professional who puts in an eight-hour day.

FOREWORD

I would love to have lots of copies of this book backstage for the people who come to see me after a performance. When they tell me how much they enjoyed my playing (performers never tire of enthusiastic listeners) but are regretful that they no longer play or have never started, I'd have something tangible to offer them. I would quickly reach behind me and bring forth the perfect answer to their dilemma: Judith Oringer's *Passion for the Piano.* In fact, this is the perfect book for anyone who has ever had even a passing interest in this curious, inanimate object called the piano.

And now I must stop delaying what I know will be your own passionate involvement in *Passion for the Piano.*

André Watts

Piano playing is a dangerous life. It must be lived dangerously. Take chances, take what comes. The world hates a coward. Who can always play safe? Who wants to? Plunge, give yourself entirely to your art and to your audiences. No one can resist that. And if you don't lose five pounds and ten drops of blood, you haven't played a concert.

Artur Rubinstein (*My Many Years*)

Prelude

The piano is a lovely instrument. You must fall in love with it, with its sound, and then be tender with it to make it, in turn, be sweeter to you. Herein lies divine beauty.

Anton Rubinstein (nineteenth-century pianist and composer)

He who plays the piano keeps sane.

Italian proverb

PRELUDE

The piano cuts a bold, romantic figure in our age of anxiety. It is a commanding, distinctive instrument—a strong solo voice in the nuclear wilderness of our century's final quarter. The piano demands of its partner a person with strong individuality, strength of character, and emotional range. Who else could handle such an imposing, versatile, attention-getting instrument? Yet this very same superstar piano can also be the best possible low-key harmonizer, amiably uniting those who sing, dance, play instruments, or simply listen.

There *is* a passion for the piano that's sweeping across the land. I first began to notice the passion for the piano phenomenon about three years ago. One of its first manifestations was visual: people began to wear keyboard scarves and T-shirts. Before long, shops were carrying piano cards, piano pads and pens, coffee mugs, keyboard ashtrays, and other piano paraphernalia. Piano images were being used in

magazine ads, on television, and in store windows to sell everything from breakfast cereal to Chanel. Besides the material evidence, the following facts also attested to a widespread passion for the piano:

There are 18 million nonprofessional pianists in this country. Nearly one out of twenty people plays the piano.

A quarter of a million new pianos are bought every year in the United States, and nearly one million old pianos are sold.

In 1982, the piano industry amounted to a half billion dollars worth of sales. This included acoustic (standard) as well as electric pianos.

There are 30 million pianos in America.

The "return to the piano" is a common occurrence, according to piano teachers and music schools. Tens of thousands of former pianists are going back to the piano bench, joining the ranks of children and other brand-new pianists.

Pianos and keyboards have proliferated to such an extent and are used for so many purposes that they have now surpassed guitars and stringed instruments in sales, and are considered the wave of the future for composition and performance.

Although I was a graduate of the High School of Music & Art in New York City, and a piano student at the Manhattan School of Music, I didn't take notice of the piano phenomenon around me until 1980, when I began to manage a concert pianist: my mother. I am continually inspired and dazzled by the pianists I hear and see. This book is dedicated to them, as well as to piano tuners, manufacturers, builders, rebuilders, students, teachers, piano dropouts, and worshippers—everyone who has a passion for the piano. *Passion for the Piano* is a celebration of the piano. I hope it will inspire you.

Judith Oringer
New York City
March 1983

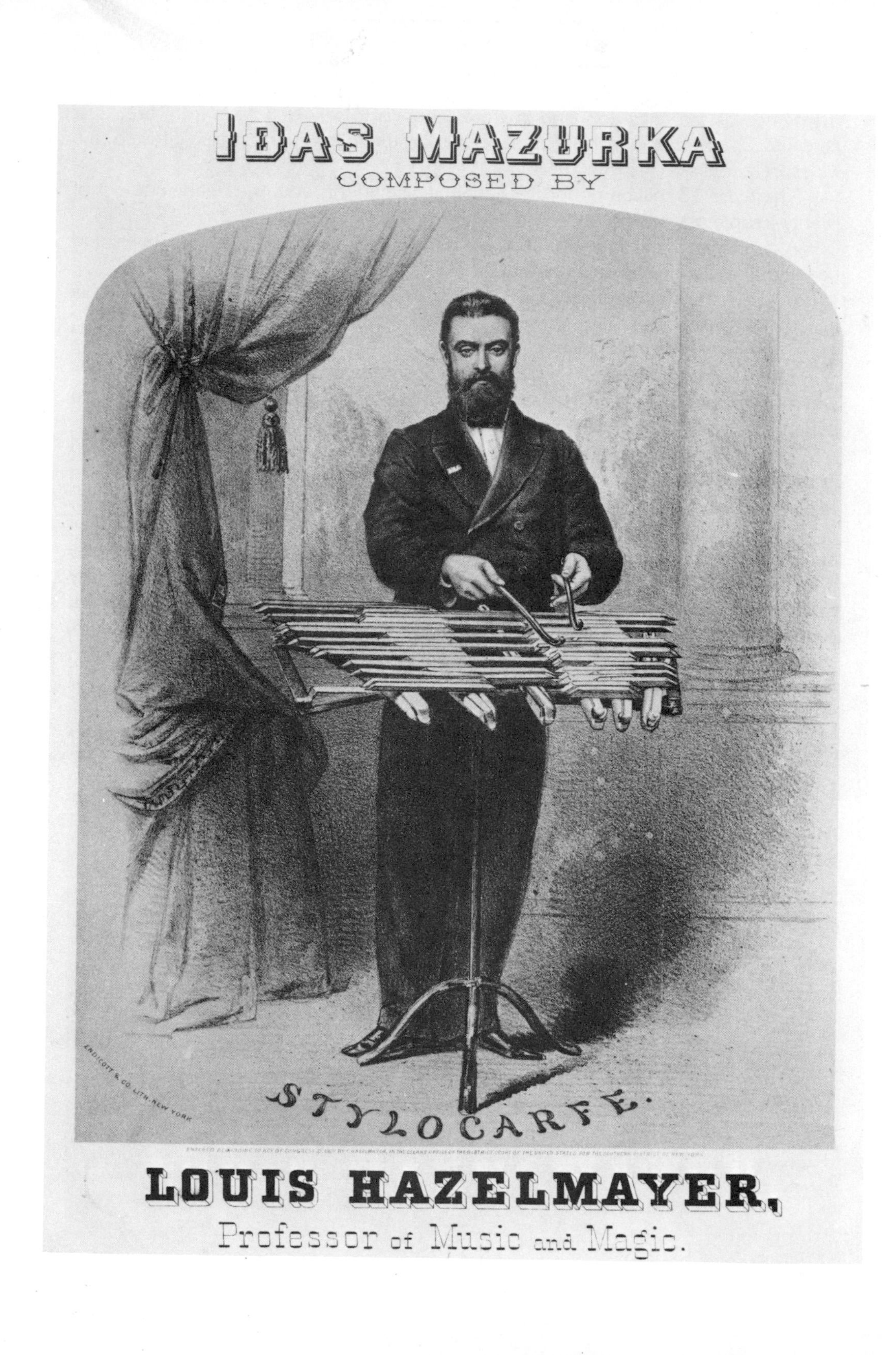
IDAS MAZURKA
COMPOSED BY
STYLOCARFE.
ENDICOTT & CO. LITH. NEW YORK
LOUIS HAZELMAYER,
Professor of Music and Magic.

1

THE PIANO

Respect the pianoforte! It gives a single man command over something complete: in its ability to go from very soft to very loud in one and the same register it excels all other instruments. The trumpet can blare, but not sigh; the flute is contrary; the pianoforte can do both. Its range embraces the highest and lowest practicable notes. Respect the pianoforte!

Ferrucio Busoni (nineteenth-century Italian composer)

I think the acoustic piano will be here for many years to come. I wouldn't venture to say it will be here forever. . . . Someone may come up with something in the electronic field that has all the absolute qualities of the piano and something else . . . in terms of self-expression. But until that happens, I think the acoustic instrument is unique—it is still the one instrument that can express everything for me.

Billy Taylor (contemporary jazz pianist and composer)

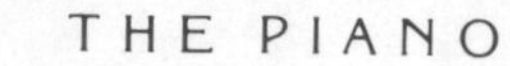

The Evolution of the Piano: From Organ to Synthesizer

The piano, so modest and unprepossessing in its original form next to the exquisite harpsichord and virginal, has become, in time, the keyboard instrument of choice. Representing the height of ingenious design and engineering principles, the piano has a power, dynamic range, and expressiveness that no previous or current keyboard instrument can match. As George Bernard Shaw stated, "Its invention was to music what the invention of printing was to poetry."

Possibly the piano's closest ancestor, the **dulcimer** originated in Persia or Assyria and appeared in Western Europe in the twelfth century. Belonging to the **zither** family of stringed instruments, the dulcimer consists of a soundbox over which strings are stretched and plucked. Today it is popular at folk festivals and jamborees for its sweet, mellow tone.

Shaped like a trapezoid, the **psaltery** is an ancient instrument with a flat soundboard over which a number of strings were stretched and plucked with a plectrum, a metal device resembling a guitar pick.

The **monochord,** a primitive stringed instrument of the Middle Ages, developed into a multi-stringed instrument with a musical bridge to establish pitch. It was used in medieval singing schools to teach intervals and to provide choirs with desired pitch levels.

Appalachian plucked dulcimer, circa 1850

American hammered dulcimer, circa 1835

Radio City Music Hall's "Mighty Wurlitzer"

South German chamber organ, 1758

The **organ** was the first keyboard instrument but, unlike its successors, uses pipes rather than strings to produce its sound.

Popular in the eighteenth century for its sweet musical tone, the **clavichord** was known as the "poor man's clavier" because of its structural simplicity in comparison to the more ornate harpsichord. Although it was the first keyed instrument to enable the performer to create subtle dynamic modulations and even a kind of vibrato, its crude construction did not allow for notes to be sustained without constant depression of the keys. The clavichord has recently been reintroduced, slightly modified, and is even available in do-it yourself kits.

A brilliant, glittery showpiece, the **harpsichord** was an aristocratic instrument made to be played in public and in halls, theaters, and royal courts. Its plucked strings create a sharp, silvery sound, which is relatively harsh next to the mellifluous-sounding piano and clavichord. Once the piano was invented, the harpsichord was pushed aside, although there has been a resurgence of interest in it in modern times.

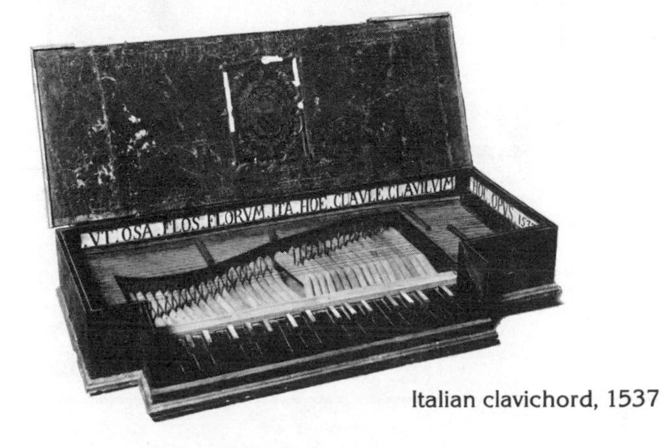

Italian clavichord, 1537

THE DEVELOPMENT

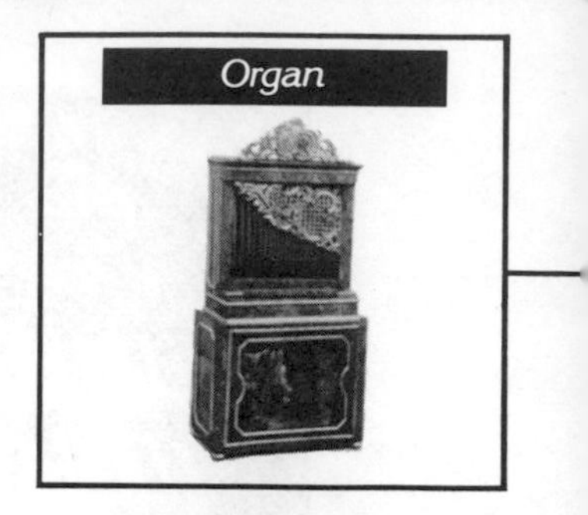

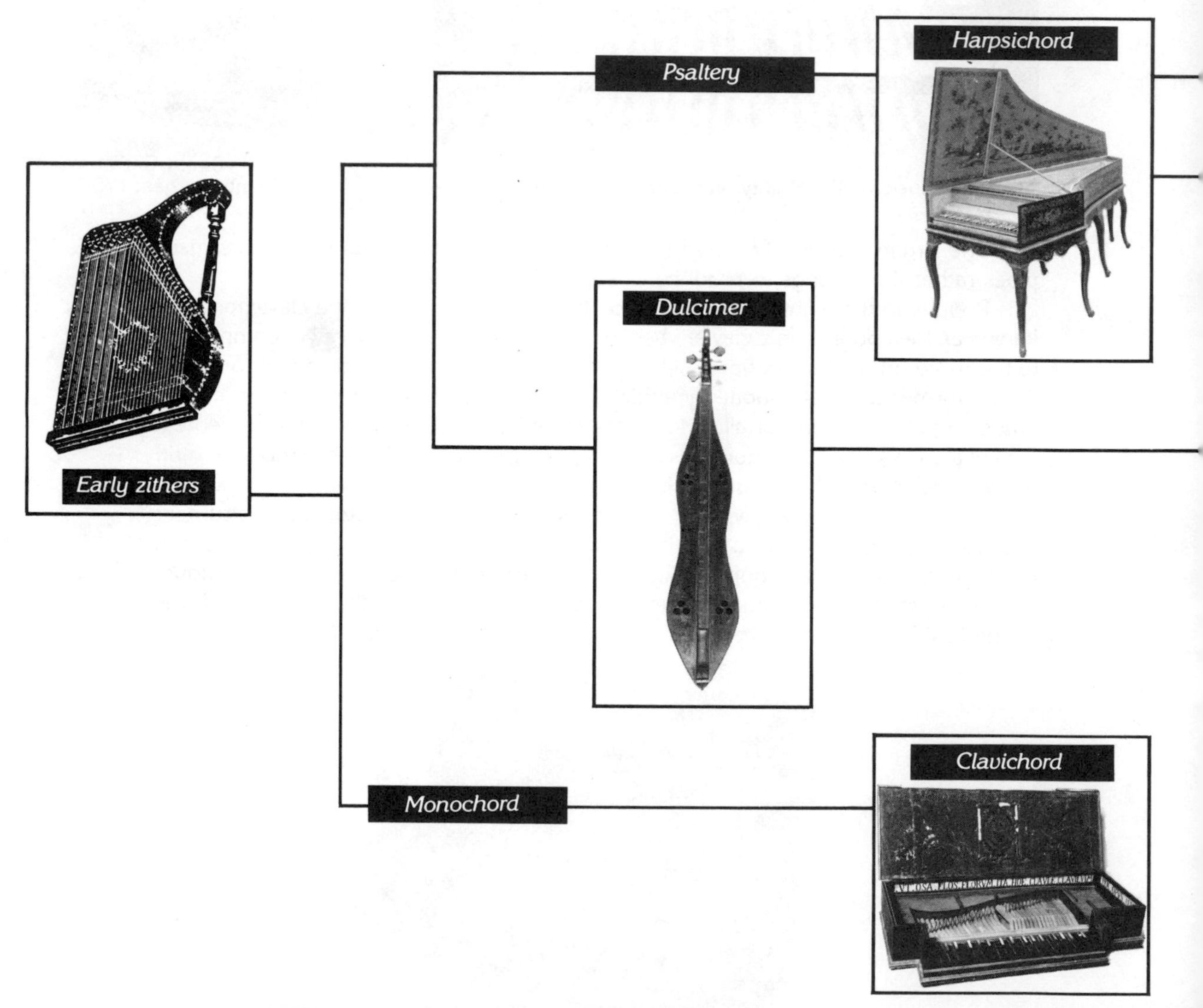

O F T H E P I A N O

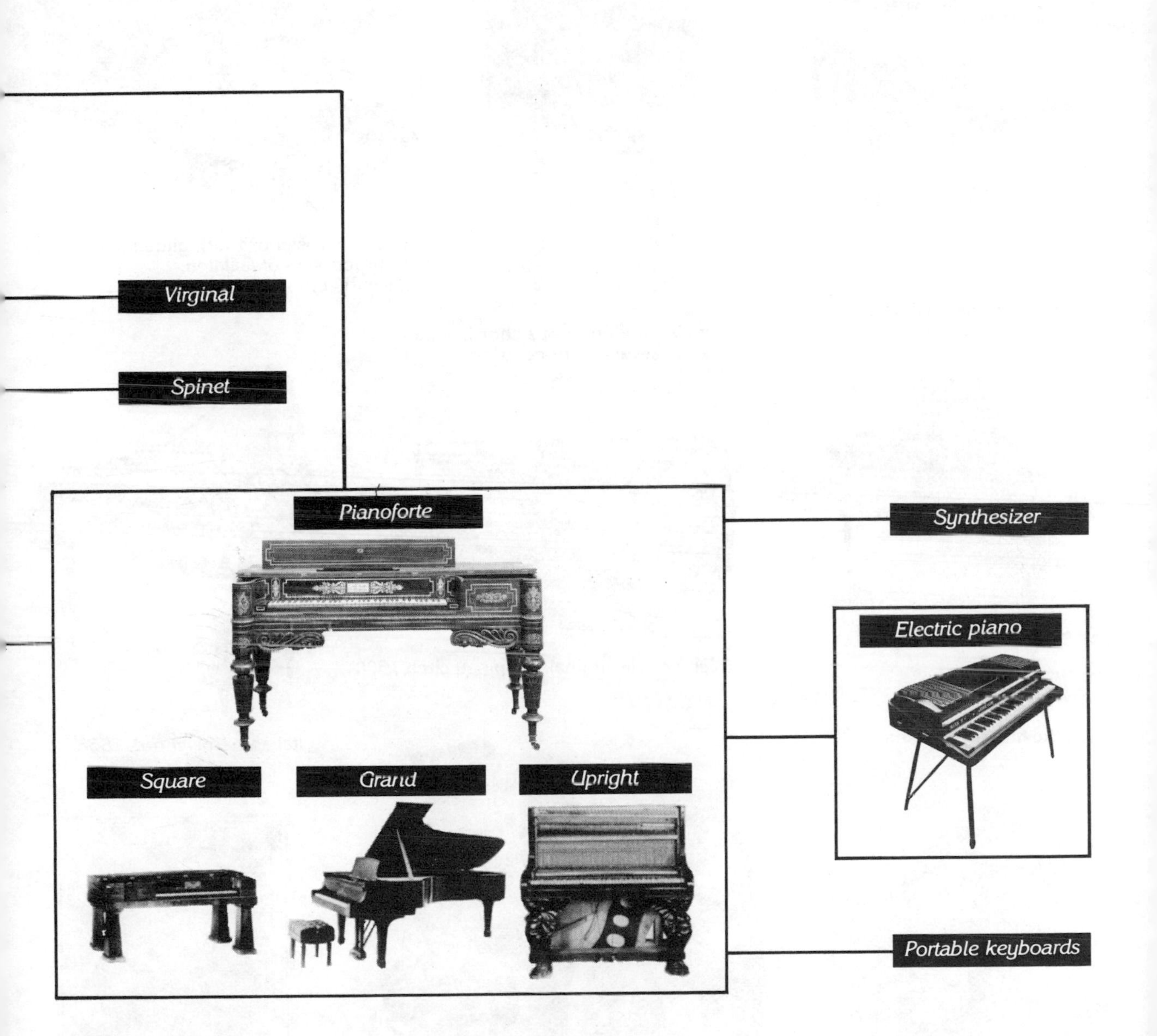
Virginal
Spinet
Pianoforte
Square
Grand
Upright
Synthesizer
Electric piano
Portable keyboards

Goermans harpsichord, eighteenth century

Italian upright harpsichord, early seventeenth century

Italian harpsichord with gilded relief of procession of Galatea, seventeenth century

One of the first pianofortes, 1720

Flemish double virginal, or spinet, circa 1600

Italian harpsichord, 1658

Moravian clavichord of 1795

Organ grinder

A small harpsichord

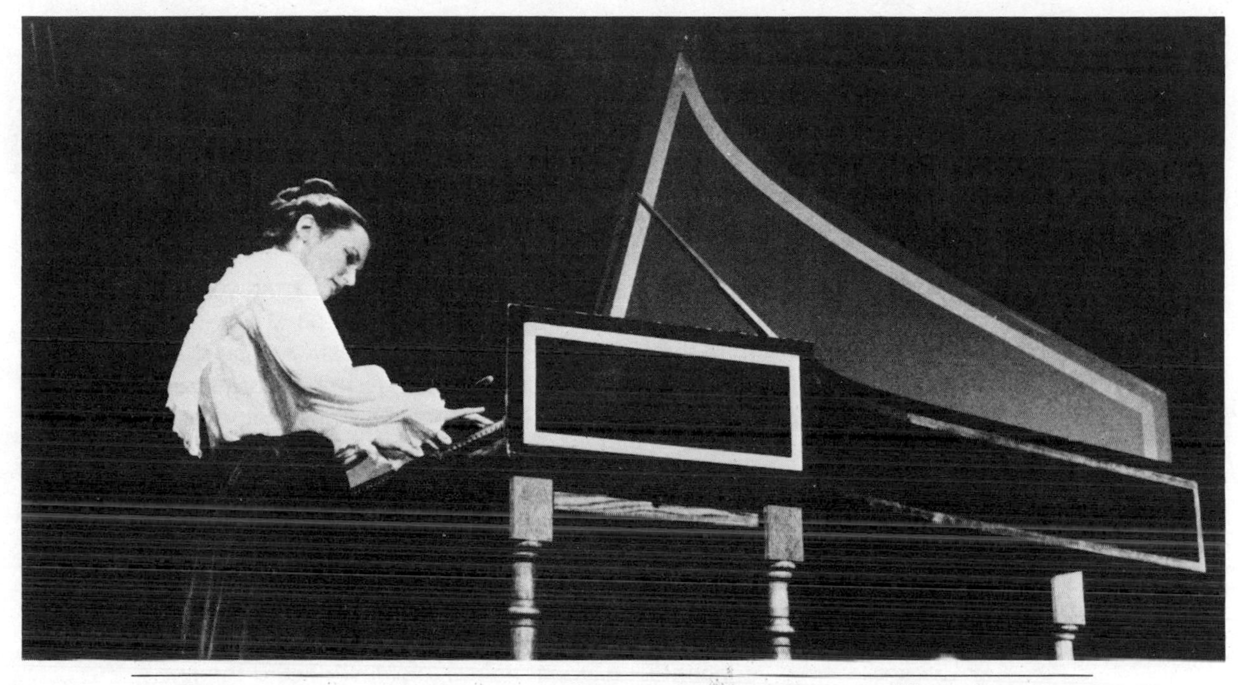

Elaine Camparone

THE BIRTH OF THE PIANO

In his attempt to make a better harpsichord, Bartolommeo Cristofori (1655–1731) discovered an entirely different instrument: the piano. Considered to be the piano's earliest inventor, he was originally a harpsichord maker who served in the Florentine court of Ferdinand de' Medici as custodian of all musical instruments. About 1709, Cristofori decided to substitute hammers in place of jacks. The use of hammers made it possible to create soft and loud sounds directly by finger pressure, which was impossible on the harpsichord. He called the invention *gravicembalo col piano e forte,* literally, harpsichord soft and loud. This was abbreviated to *pianoforte,* then to *piano.* Cristofori came up with three principles still used by piano makers today. Besides inventing hammers, he developed an escapement device to permit the hammer to drop back immediately after delivering its string a blow, leaving the string to vibrate freely as long as the key is held. Cristofori also invented the shifting soft pedal arrangement, called the *una corda.* These substitutions may have seemed minor at first, and the earliest piano looked like a harpsichord and was fitted into a harpsichord case. Its familiar look disguised its unfamiliar novelties and reassured prospective buyers. Although the early piano had fifty-four notes compared to the modern piano's eighty-eight, it had all the other essentials: wire strings, keys, hammers, dampers, and escapement. Cristofori's original pianos—he made about twenty in his lifetime—represented the keyboard instrument's leap into the future.

TOWARD THE PIANO OF TODAY

Although the piano was an Italian invention, it was the German, Austrian, English, and French instrument makers who would come up with design and structural improvements and acoustic changes that would greatly improve the piano's capacity, making for its unconditional victory over the harpsichord and all other keyboard instruments by the end of the eighteenth century. Indeed, as philosopher Jacques Barzun has stated: "More than any other music-making contrivance, the piano's development has paralleled that of technology." Various mechanical improvements followed in the next century and a half. Gottfried Silbermann of Germany built many of the early pianos, including those that Johann Sebastian Bach heard and criticized. Bach, however, did not foresee any real future for the piano; he was an organist at heart, and a conservative man. Years later, when he was shown a piano that incorporated many of his suggestions, he admitted that the piano was coming along.

Andreas Stein of Germany came from the Viennese school of piano making. From the 1780s on he produced a lighter, simpler piano. Mozart played the Stein fortepiano, a light piano with a rippling action. Mozart had only begun to concentrate on the piano after a trip to Paris in 1777 at age twenty-one. But given his genius, it's not surprising that his mother was soon to write to his father that "he plays differently than he does at Salzburg, because here they have pianofortes everywhere and he knows how to handle these so incomparably that nobody has ever heard the like." Mozart became the first great virtuoso of the piano and led the way in championing his chosen keyboard instrument.

John Broadwood, of England, made pianos from 1770 on. He invented the sustaining pedal, strengthened the case and strings to increase volume, and added an

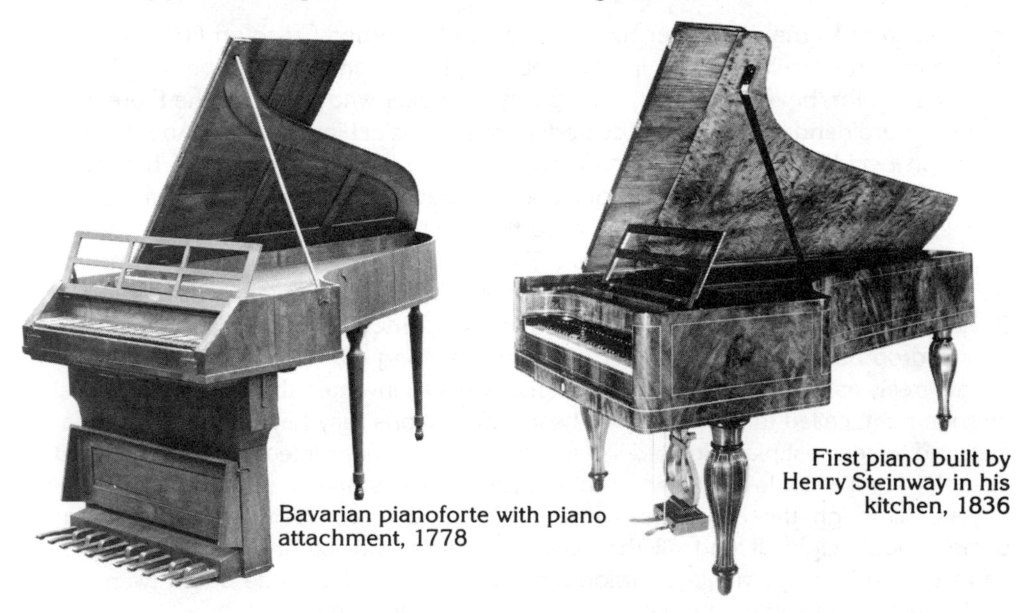

Bavarian pianoforte with piano attachment, 1778

First piano built by Henry Steinway in his kitchen, 1836

The ornate Erard piano, circa 1830

octave, extending the piano's keyboard range to six octaves. Beethoven preferred the Broadwood for its substantiality—but even on these he would snap the strings continuously and entangle the hammers. Beethoven begged a fellow musician to remove the broken strings and disengage the hammers as he played. The man later said: "My job was harder than his, for I had constantly to jump to the right, to the left, to run around the piano to get at all the troubles." Beethoven was playing and writing for pianos that couldn't fulfill his need for powerful expression—in fact, he was composing for a piano that didn't yet exist. This passion demanded that a new instrument be born, and it was. Beethoven actually changed the way the piano was played as well as how music was written.

Sebastian Erard, a French piano maker who fled to England for political reasons in the early 1820s, was responsible for several ingenious inventions in the piano's development. He perfected the double escapement mechanism, which allows notes to be repeated quickly, invented foot pedals for the soft-loud function (formerly knee operated), and used iron braces to strengthen the frame and accommodate greater string tension.

The Industrial Revolution further advanced the technology of the piano. The iron frame was introduced to replace the piano's original wood frame, enabling it to support a string tension of eighteen to twenty tons, far greater than ever before.

Today's piano is built on many of the design and structural principles of the Steinway piano built in the latter part of the nineteenth century. That piano incorporated the following breakthroughs: the overstrung scale, a cross-stringing procedure whereby the long bass strings crossed over the shorter ones—a dramatic economization of space—and a full cast-iron plate. More recent Steinway innovations included an accelerated, improved action, and a diaphragmatic sounding board, which pro-

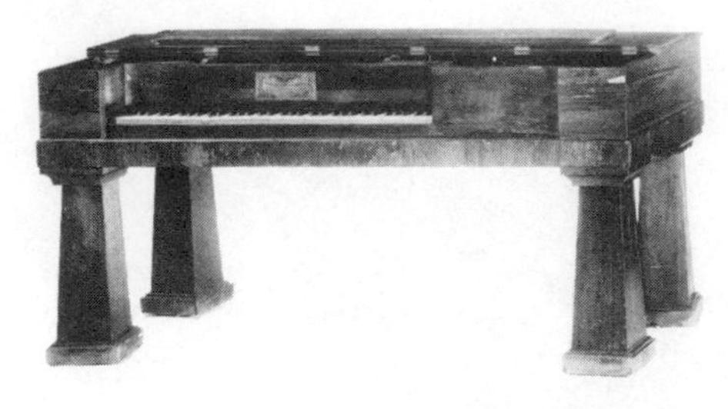

American square piano, circa 1840

Baltimore upright, 1858

Custom-made Sohmer piano

vided uniform tonal quality. By 1880, the piano had assumed the form we know today.

Although the operating principles remain the same, the technology of the modern piano has changed to accommodate new situations and different demands. Not only does it have to hold up under rock, jazz, and classical pianists, the piano is flown on airplanes, exposed to pollution, and faces other contemporary situations. Even though it is always being improved, the piano retains its essence, perfected over a century ago.

Piano making proved to be fertile ground for imaginative experimentation. Most piano creations lasted for a few years, then disappeared completely. Square pianos in outrageously fancy styles were abundant, as were round, oval, and hexagonal pianos. There was the double piano, in which two pianos were eternally joined, the writing desk piano, in which the keyboard could be pushed in and out like a drawer, and a pianoforte-bed, displayed at a London exhibition in 1851, which started to play by itself when one lay down on it.

ACOUSTIC AND ELECTRONIC: WELCOME TO THE FUTURE!

There will always be pianists to carry on the classical traditions in music. But as we approach the twenty-first century, many are seeking the new, almost limitless sounds of the electronic frontier. Electronic musical instruments, the children of the second

Devo

keyboard revolution, can create musical and nonmusical sounds such as those of a full orchestra, the helicopters in the film *Apocalypse Now*, and oceans and birds.

The two most important electronic instrument families in this "brave new world" are:

THE SYNTHESIZER. Considered to be one of the most revolutionary musical developments of the twentieth century, the synthesizer was pioneered in the early 1960s by experimental instrument makers and musicians such as Bob Moog, Allan R. Pearlman, and Donald Buchla. The synthesizer is designed to reconstruct the complex waveforms of musical sound. Its sound source is provided by oscillators which create the basic wave forms, added to or subtracted from, to produce sounds.

The synthesizer can record, store, and manipulate any acoustic sound, and, thanks to its electronic filter, can create a piano melody one minute and a vocal choir or violin the next. It can also be hooked up to a computer, which would enable you to create a personal sound library of romantic piano nocturnes, train whistles, barking dogs, and exotic birdcalls.

Of the two types of synthesizers available today, analog and digital, the latter is considered to be state of the art. It can remember any programmed sound, edit and store acoustic sounds, and print out complete orchestral scores, and it has unlimited sonic possibilities.

Many advanced keyboard players, including virtuoso acoustic pianists such as Oscar Peterson and Herbie Hancock, are fascinated by synthesizers and their future. Synthesizers were originally huge and extremely expensive, but with technology's

A Synclavier II

rapid advance they have become small and portable, and can be purchased for about $5000. Two of the most advanced synthesizer systems, the Synclavier, made by New England Digital Corp., and the Fairlight CMI, of Fairlight Distributors, have standard keyboards with contacts arranged to produce a digital code, keyboards resembling a typewriter, visual display units for programming, and data storage systems.

"I'm very attracted to orchestral colors. So, for me, my synthesizers are tools for creating new instrumental sounds," says jazz pianist and innovative composer Herbie Hancock. "The body and the shape of a synthesizer have nothing to do with the sound. There's no acoustic chamber, so it's lightweight—you can carry a synthesizer with you." As synthesizers are being made visually more attractive, the piano player, Hancock says, can play a synthesizer on stage and not mind the way it looks. He foresees the development in the near future of a synthesizer that works and sounds exactly like a piano, but weighs far less—like the electric grand piano. It will, he thinks, probably sound adequate for certain kinds of applications, "but I wouldn't expect André Watts to play an electric grand piano."

The synthesizer awaits composers and orchestrators to do justice to its capabilities. Classical pianist Lorin Hollander asks, "Who knows where it's all going? These are viable sounds being produced which have a tremendous emotional impact. We shall have to wait for the Bach of this era, who is going to take all of them and create something extraordinary."

THE ELECTRIC PIANO. This instrument was built to make the piano more manageable, more portable, and more amplified. No longer is the poor pianist saddled with an out of tune disaster or unable to bring his piano with him to a performance.

The electric piano is wired to an amplifier and uses pickups, a type of microphone that is physically attached to the instrument. Any acoustic piano can be

Rhodes electric piano

converted to an electric piano by means of pickups. (An electronic piano, on the other hand, produces sounds by means of oscillators.) Most rock and many jazz groups use some kind of electric piano. Some of the most popular types of electric pianos are:

The Fender Rhodes. It has keys and hammers, like the acoustic piano, but lacks strings or a sounding board. This piano has a bell-like quality which works well in jazz or rock. Most major rock groups have a place in their keyboard "rig" for a Fender Rhodes.

The Clavinet. This piano does have strings located under each note, and works like an electric guitar. The clavinet has a percussive, funky quality. Stevie Wonder often uses it on his albums. Its characteristic sound is warm and mellow.

The Hohner Pianet. The Hohner Pianet doesn't require a power supply, which is why you can take it out to sea with you.

Yamaha Electric Grand. Although this piano has strings, it also has pickups, and the absence of a sounding board makes it easy to transport. This is a breakthrough instrument since it can produce a decent piano sound yet is light and portable.

The Casio. Casios are fun, easy to play, and quite inexpensive. Completely different from any other electronic instrument, they are actually musical models mathematically represented and stored on chips.

A Hohner pianet at sea

SPACE-AGE ELECTRONIC COMPANIES

If you are interested in purchasing or in learning more about electronic instruments, the following are the principal manufacturers of synthesizers, electronic pianos, organs, and other electronic instruments and devices:

CASIO, 15 Gardner Road, Fairfield, NJ 07006

DIGITAL KEYBOARDS, 105 Fifth Avenue, Garden City Park, NY 11040

HAMMOND ORGAN COMPANY, 4200 W. Diversey Ave., Chicago, IL 60639

HOHNER, Andrews Road, Hicksville, NY 11802

KORG, Unicord, Westbury, NY 11590

MARANTZ PIANO COMPANY, P.O. Box 460, Morganton, NC 28655

MOOG MUSIC, 2500 Walden Avenue, Buffalo, NY 14225

NEW ENGLAND DIGITAL CORP., Box 546, White River Junction, VT 05001

OBERHEIM, 2250 S. Barrington Avenue, Los Angeles, CA 90064

OTARI, 2 Davis Drive, Belmont, CA 94002

RHODES, 1300 E. Valencia Drive, Fullerton, CA 92631

ROLAND, 1022 S. La Cienega Blvd., Los Angeles, CA 90035

SEQUENTIAL CIRCUITS, 3051 N. First St., San Jose, CA 95134

Space-age keyboard

THE GREAT DEBATE: ACOUSTIC VERSUS ELECTRONIC

Comparing the merits of acoustic and electronic instruments raises controversy among musicians. There are classical musicians who fear the worst—being replaced by a big synthesized box—and there are those who have no interest in this electronic future. To them, the acoustic piano is unmatched and unmatchable, and that's where their hearts—and future—remain. Still, other pianists draw from the best of both the acoustic and electronic worlds, grateful that the acoustic piano introduced them to keyboard instruments in the first place.

Steve Gaboury

"Not a day goes by without my thanking my lucky stars that I was born into the piano," reflects jazz/blues keyboardist Steve Gaboury, music director for Angela Bofill.

Herbie Hancock still feels closely tied to the acoustic piano and considers himself basically an acoustic pianist "because, to me, it's the daddy of it all." He adds, "The piano has developed for more than 250 years, and so has the repertoire. It's a natural part of Western music. Synthesizers haven't gotten to that point yet."

The Who keyboardist, Tim Gorman, feels that the fate of any instrument—acoustic or electronic—depends on writers and producers, on artistry rather than on technology. "Technology will always be there. There's a lot of technology that goes into making an acoustic piano, probably more than making a synthesizer. But whether it's a piano or a synthesizer, it's got to be played. If no one writes for it and keeps it alive as a viable musical form, the instrument will die."

Steve Gaboury feels it's a fantastic age in which to be a keyboard player—"Why, if Bach were alive today, he'd be freaking out about synthesizers! To him, the organ was that: the presynthesizer synthesizer. He'd certainly have tried it out. But the piano has an affinity to it. If you lined up all great music, it could be written on the piano. You can look at all the notes, play the chords, hear the strings, drums, bass, the whole orchestra. It is soft, touch-sensitive, and has a huge repertoire."

Peter Schott, of Kid Creole and the Coconuts, comes from a German family that was one of Beethoven's publishers. Schott feels that the keyboard, including the acoustic piano, will be the critical instrument for the future for two main reasons: a keyboard falls perfectly under the hand, and one can adapt theory and harmony on it without any problem. "Now there are more instruments for the keyboard player," he says. "You can go into the synthesizer realm, and you'll have the whole orchestra at your fingertips. Did you see *Close Encounters of the Third Kind*? There was interstellar communication in that movie—they used a keyboard to communicate with the extraterrestrials!"

Glenn Gould understood the synthesizer's potential and was attracted to the electronic experience to the exclusion of the "live" concert. He declared in 1964 that "the concert is dead" and stopped giving performances altogether. He claimed he never went to a concert after 1967. If concerts were a thing of the past for Gould, records were the wave of the future. "Recording for me is not a picture postcard of a concert. . . . Recordings are, to a certain degree, timeless. They are something outside of history, outside of a particular environmental context." He often compared their relationship to concerts as films were to stage performances—a different phenomenon entirely.

Classical pianist Misha Dichter holds the opposite view from Gould's about concerts, although he too loves the scope of recordings. "Sounds are coming out as the technology increases that have nothing at all to do with concerts any more," he

Glenn Gould

says. "Suddenly the piano is now 100 feet long against an orchestra and you, by virtue of technology, can drown out a brass section in a Liszt concerto. Pretty good!" Recordings are a joy for Dichter. "It gives us the luxury we don't have as performers of playing a phrase over we're not terribly pleased with. Imagine saying to an audience, 'I can do it better, just hold on a minute and I'll try it again.' " But he feels recordings can "spoil you to death," and notices how careful his very first concerts are after he's made a record. "But you *must* get out of that cycle, you *must* play concerts," he asserts.

Chick Corea is a jazz composer-pianist who experiments musically in both the acoustic and electronic ranges. For Corea, "The acoustic piano is this very, very interesting tool which is probably one of the more complex nonelectric machines I've ever seen. There's so much life in it, so much has been invested in it. I don't know if the piano will ever be very much improved upon. It's so workable as it is. You can put ten fingers on it—you know what I mean? It can be a solo instrument, a group instrument, a teacher's tool, a composer's tool. Even in contemporary life, there are so many great pianists. If someone was a composer, I don't see how they could neglect the instrument. There's so much music that moves through the piano."

Corea gets great joy from playing the piano. "I can have so much fun by myself—I'm not sure how much fun a flute player can have before having to play with

Chick Corea

another flute—or a piano. I can have a ball for days and weeks and not ever come close to another instrument." He says that this may be one of the keys to the piano's popularity, "because any new creative idea is thought from an individual mind. Groups don't create ideas; individuals do. When a musician is working out his ideas, he uses the piano. And he can do it himself!"

As the lines between the acoustic and electronic and the classical and more contemporary musical forms become blurred, many pianists have a passionate interest in several worlds simultaneously. Film and TV composer Bob James, for instance, is torn between his love for the acoustic piano and for the synthesizer. "At least fifty percent of me now is equally stimulated by pursuing the whole area of synthesizer keyboard music, while the other fifty percent is saying, come on back and enjoy the beauty of the grand piano. Because no matter how much experimenting I do, neither ends up being any more elegant, exciting, or inspiring than the infinite number of tonal shadings that you can get the best out of the acoustic piano. I like both worlds—both challenges. I don't like to give either up."

One musician who sums up the acoustic/electric question rather neatly is Lyle Mays of the Pat Metheny jazz group. "I use electronic keyboards, devices, everything," Lyle says. "But when it comes to expressing myself, I can only do it on the piano. Part of the reason is that the piano has evolved for so long. The other instruments are babies—they haven't gone through enough development yet. They don't have enough tools to really allow an individual to express himself. I always come back to the piano. The piano's no dinosaur. I think that the different electronic instruments will make the piano more and more special—they'll validate acoustic pianos. I think there's room for as many instruments as possible," Mays affirms, concluding, "Pianos will last forever!"

Lyle Mays

PIANO SUPERLATIVES

One of Bartolommeo Cristofori's original pianofortes, dating from 1720, is still in existence and is on display at the Metropolitan Museum of Art's Rare Instrument Collection in New York City.

● The highest price ever paid for a piano is $390,000, for a Steinway grand built in 1884. It is considered a masterpiece of nineteenth-century design and workmanship. Called the "Alma-Tadema piano," it was named for the British painter who supervised the opulent decoration on its Steinway body. The piano has ivory, coral, and mother-of-pearl inlay and carved lions for legs. It was built to decorate the Madison Avenue mansion of the then-president of the Metropolitan Museum of Art. It was sold on March 26, 1980, at Sotheby Park Bernet, New York City, for the Martin Beck Theatre, and was bought by a non-pianist as an investment.

● The grandest grand piano ever built weighed one and one-third tons (the average grand weighs about 1000 pounds). It was eleven feet, eight inches long, and was made in 1935 by Charles H. Challen & Son Ltd. of London.

● The tensile strength on the piano's frame—the tremendous pull that is trapped inside the average piano—is capable of powering a hoist that could lift forty or more heavy old uprights simultaneously.

● A recent survey shows that there are over 18 million amateur pianists; seventy-nine percent of those are female; and twenty-one percent, male. The players' median age is twenty-eight.

● Organ building became so elaborate that, at Winchester Cathedral in England in the tenth century, an organ was built that had 400 pipes and twenty-six bellows, needed seventy men to blow it, and more than one player.

The $390,000 Alma-Tadema piano

Piano Manufacturing

The piano manufacturing business has seen dramatic changes in the twentieth century, particularly over the last twenty years. In 1900, there were 7000 piano manufacturers in America, including families who made pianos in their homes. One out of every six people in America was involved in some aspect of the piano business, including the production of raw or man-made materials used in constructing a piano. Today, however, there are only about ten independent piano manufacturers and just six major piano companies. A far cry from the mom-and-pop piano makers of the past, these are Steinway, Baldwin, Sohmer, Kimball, Wurlitzer, and Aeolian. Despite the transition from family to corporate ownership, the hand craftsmanship and pride in the product seem to have prevailed. Combined with the most modern business and manufacturing techniques, the piano industry in the 1980s is unique—and healthy, if somewhat pared down.

According to the National Piano Manufacturers Association and industry estimates, piano manufacturing is a half-billion-dollar-a-year industry. In 1982, 203,000 American-made pianos were sold in the United States, a slight decrease over the past two to three years, but an overall increase over a ten-year period.

The Yamaha factory

Steinway grand piano frames

The sales figures of new American instruments tell only part of the story. Piano manufacturers say that the secondhand piano business is doing remarkably well, and they estimate that nearly 1 million used pianos are sold in America yearly.

In the past decade the American piano industry has been faced with intense competition from the Koreans and the Japanese, the latter having already cornered twenty percent of the American market with Yamaha and Kawai pianos. In fact, in Hamamatsu, Japan, where the Yamaha is manufactured, more pianos are made per year than in any other part of the world. But United States piano manufacturers have risen quickly to the challenge. Piano companies are rapidly increasing their know-how in engineering as well as in marketing and manufacturing. These firms are developing more efficient, profitable methods, and new products that the public can more easily afford, such as the practical spinet, a much smaller and cheaper piano than a grand.

The two basic types of pianos are grands and uprights. Grand pianos are constructed on a horizontal plane, which means that the strings are stretched horizontally across the plate and framework, and come in three sizes: a baby grand is four and a half feet to six feet long; a medium grand, six to eight feet long; and a concert grand, eight to nine feet long and sometimes longer. While only five percent of the pianos manufactured today are grand pianos, they are played and featured most often because they tend to be far more responsive and powerful than uprights.

Upright pianos, also called vertical pianos, have strings that are stretched vertically across the plate and framework. Uprights vary in height: a full-size is forty-eight inches or more; the studio model is forty-four inches; the console is thirty-nine to forty-two inches; and a spinet, popular because of its small size, is thirty-six to thirty-eight inches. Upright pianos have two major types of actions: direct blow action and drop action. Direct blow action makes for a better piano because the action is mounted above the ends of the keys, allowing direct movement of the parts, a strong hammer blow, and maximum tonal response. Drop action, mounted behind and below the keys, sacrifices sound and is harder to fix because the space is so cramped.

Today, there is a slowly developing renaissance in piano making. With the high cost of new pianos, many people are buying used pianos and having them rebuilt or refinished. At least a dozen companies in New York City alone are now starting to rebuild old pianos, which are being sent from all over the country. Trained piano makers are also in considerable demand.

With his own shop in New York's piano district (between 55th and 58th streets on the West Side), Kalman Detrich, a gifted piano rebuilder-technician, will open the Museum of the American Piano in 1983 to represent the evolution of piano making in America. This museum is a testimony to the reawakening of interest in the secrets of piano making and to the unique properties and qualities of the modern piano, a profound cultural achievement.

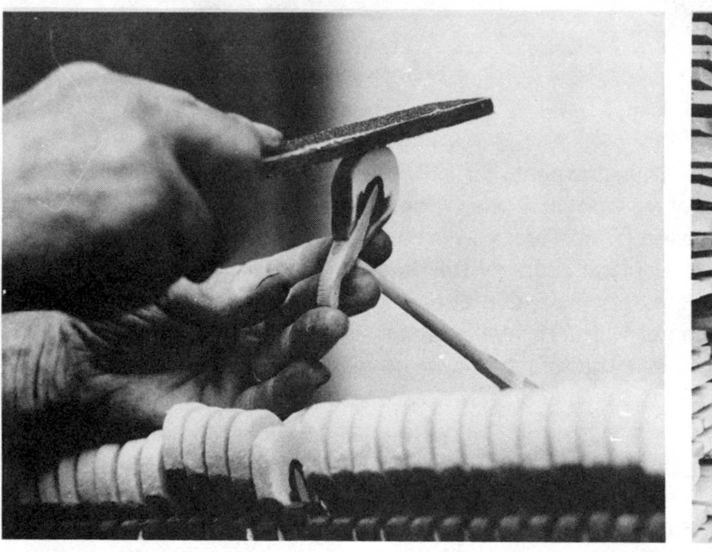

THE MAKING OF A PIANO

The Steinway factory lies across the East River from Manhattan, in Long Island City, where 400 acres of farmland were bought by the Steinway family in the nineteenth century to accommodate all the lumber and raw materials needed. The factory workers used to live in the company's "Steinway Village" (there's still a Steinway Street subway station), but now the Steinway craftspeople commute to work.

A tour of the factory begins in the lumber yard, where gigantic stacks of wood are piled up according to type: poplar, walnut, sugar maple (from Vermont), mahogany (from Central America or Africa), and spruce (from California). Spruce is used for most pianos' sounding boards—the heart of a piano—because of its terrific resonance. The amount of wood found at any piano factory should come as no surprise, since a piano is ninety percent wood. The wood, left outside intentionally, is subjected

Bent wood rims of Steinway grand pianos

Franz Mohr, Steinway's chief concert technician

to all the elements. Anything that can withstand a New York winter and summer, along with rain, wind, and air pollution, has got to be made of strong stuff (sixty percent of the wood is later rejected).

A stroll down a single cavernous floor inside the factory offers the sight of pianos at every stage of creation. The most dramatic process of all is called rim-bending, during which the piano frame is bent into its graceful piano shape. It takes six strong people to bend the wood, ever so gently, but firmly, and quickly, too, since they have only twelve minutes to bend the rim before the glue starts to adhere.

Walking through a good piano factory is probably like walking back in time. Nineteenth-century pride in craftsmanship is combined with advanced scientific laboratory techniques. Piano craftspeople are usually immersed in very detailed functions, such as laminating the wood, "bellying" the piano—fitting and gluing the soundboard into the case to provide maximum amplification for the string vibrations—polishing, and tone regulating. Tone regulators, the élite of the factory, begin their work when the piano is essentially built; they must bring it to life. Ray Perada, a master tone regulator, gets very emotional about his pianos, and his pride in them is visible. "This is my life. I'm in love with my work. I'm not just saying this. I do feel the piano has a personality of its own."

While there is no assembly line, there are machines that contribute to the overall design; among the few are fork lifts and planing devices, as well as ultramodern innovations such as the acoustically controlled chambers that deaden the sound so that the tone regulation can be done under perfectly stringent conditions.

It takes one full year to make a Steinway grand and a bit less time to construct an upright. A piano seen at various stages really looks like a Rube Goldberg contraption with its various escapements, levers, and complicated mechanisms. When put together, it is a triumph of mechanical and human genius.

PIANO MANUFACTURERS

STEINWAY. The best-known and most élite piano manufacturer in America, Steinway & Sons was founded in New York in 1853. The first Steinway piano was made in the kitchen of founder Henry Steinway in Seesen, Germany, in 1836. (Steinway changed the family name from Steinweg when he emigrated to America in 1850.)

The modern Steinway has the same basic designs, engineering principles, and scaling specifications (such as string lengths and tension) that were perfected in the 1870s and used as the basis for the modern piano. With no false modesty, Steinway & Sons calls its piano "the instrument of the immortals." The Steinway's reputation is based on its beautiful tone, bright sound, and power. It is used in concert halls, in music colleges, and in many homes. A popular misconception is that Steinway makes millions of pianos every year. Actually, it produces only about 4000 pianos, 3000 of which are grands. Yet Steinway pianos represent 95% of the concert market. It has made only 480,000 pianos in its entire history. (Yamaha now makes 200,000 a year.)

A Steinway baby grand costs about $13,000; an ebony concert grand (a Steinway "D"), about $31,000; and a walnut grand, $35,000. The Steinway reputation is such that people who want a Steinway will buy one, regardless of its price or of the state of the economy.

Miniature street scene, part of turn-of-the-century piano

Al Bianchi, the "million-dollar-a-year" Steinway salesman, is an example of the Steinway phenomenon. Last year, Bianchi sold a million dollars' worth of Steinway pianos to individuals.

Through its German branch in Hamburg, Steinway also manufactures and sells an excellent piano to Europe—the Hamburg Steinway.

The company was sold to CBS in 1972, which doesn't seem to have affected the world of Steinway. As John Steinway, a descendant of Steinway's founder and the board chairman, maintains, "We're just pigheaded Dutchmen who know how to make one product very well. We don't make guitars, we don't make electric pianos. We do what we do well."

BALDWIN. The Baldwin Piano & Organ Company bought out the Bechstein piano company in 1962, 100 years after it was founded. Since 1968, Baldwin has been owned by a financial holding company in Cincinnati. Baldwin produces several thousand grand and vertical pianos a year and receives twenty-five percent of the market share. The Baldwin piano is appreciated by concert artists and very much favored by jazz and popular pianists, who like its brilliant, "pingy" tone. Baldwin is the number two, "we try harder" company, and everything about it is more comfortable and less formal than the elegant, old-world ambiance of Steinway. The average Baldwin buyer is "a middle-class family with a nine-year-old daughter," says Jack Huff, division manager in the New York store.

Henry E. Steinway, by Matthew Brady

Rim bending at the Steinway factory

Steinway lumberyard, 1880s

KIMBALL. The largest American piano manufacturer, Kimball is owned by a furniture company in Indiana. Despite its comparatively high production, Kimball only manufactures one-fifth as many pianos as Yamaha. One of America's oldest piano firms, Kimball produces a good, solid piano. Its glamorous claim to fame is Bösendorfer, the prestigious Austrian piano company that Kimball International acquired in 1966. The Bösendorfer piano, like the Lippizaner Stallions, is considered a national treasure by the Austrians. Founder Ignaz Bösendorfer started his company in 1826, and Franz Liszt was an early fan of the instrument. This legendary piano is now starting to make its appearance on the American concert scene, and, along with the Steinway and the Bechstein, is very popular in Europe. It takes three and a half years to make one Bösendorfer (two years are spent just in drying out the wood). The long, involved Bösendorfer piano-making process accounts for its price, steep by any standard: $60,000 for an "Imperial" model, a nine-and-a-half-foot grand, which is six inches longer than any other piano, and has nine extra keys. It is the world's most expensive piano. The Bösendorfer is known for its beautiful, singing tone: a deep bass, clear tenor, and bell-like soprano. Most of the wood is solid spruce, which makes not only the sounding board, but the whole piano, vibrate. Oscar Peterson, Elton John, and Garrick Ohlsson, among others, play the Bösendorfer.

AEOLIAN PIANO COMPANY. Aeolian has taken over several important piano lines, and, until recently, was producing fine grand pianos—Chickering, Knabe, and Mason-Hamlin—that date back to the beginning of the American piano-manufacturing industry. The company plans to reopen its factory in the very near future. Meanwhile, it continues to produce uprights and player pianos, including the Winter, Henry F. Miller,

Bösendorfer

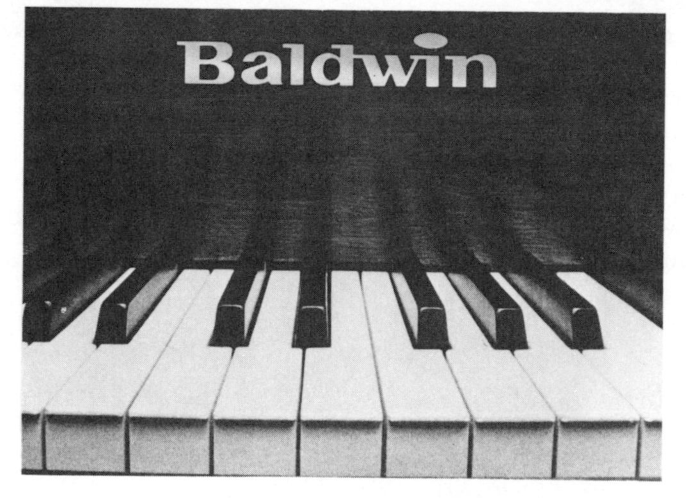

and sixty-four-note Melodigrand. Now headed by Steinway's former president, Peter Perez, Aeolian is the largest American piano manufacturer devoted exclusively to making pianos. They also manufacture their own actions, keys, and plates.

WURLITZER. This all-American piano company has a large share of the market, but is now cutting costs and focusing on efficiency to offset the decrease in piano sales of the last few years. Wurlitzer continues to make organs, on which it built its reputation.

SOHMER & CO. European piano maker Hugh Sohmer emigrated to America and founded his company in 1872. Sohmer is still a family-run business—the third generation of Sohmers is presently at the helm. Sohmer moved to Ivoryton (a perfectly named place for a piano maker!), Connecticut, in 1982, to be close to Pratt Reed, a large manufacturer of piano parts. Sohmer's reputation is based on the vertical piano, but it also manufactures baby grands. Although Sohmer is sold almost entirely to private owners, the studio upright is popular with schools and piano teachers. Sohmer used to specialize in "Hollywood pianos," and created special-order pianos with 1920s art deco or Spanish designs for movie stars such as Jean Harlow. Harry Sohmer, Sr., whose father founded the company, feels he's a "living anachronism—there are so few of us left."

YAMAHA. Yamaha, a Japanese company, produces a fine working piano, and is now trying to develop a concert grand to compete with a Steinway or Baldwin. Many rock pianists prefer the Yamaha because of its very bright sound. The Yamaha company also has a music foundation and promotes music worldwide. Yamaha wisely spends more of its budget on research and development—the basis of progress—than on advertising.

KAWAI. Its grand piano factory in Ryuyo, Japan, is one of the largest grand piano assembly plants in the world. Scientists at the plant study the creation of sound. Kawai is a fifty-year-old family-owned business. Jazz pianists such as Joanne Brackeen and Chuck Mangione, as well as the inimitable Steve Allen, prefer Kawais. The company compares its piano-making process to taming a wild horse or breaking in a new car, followed by tuning and mechanical adjustments for perfection.

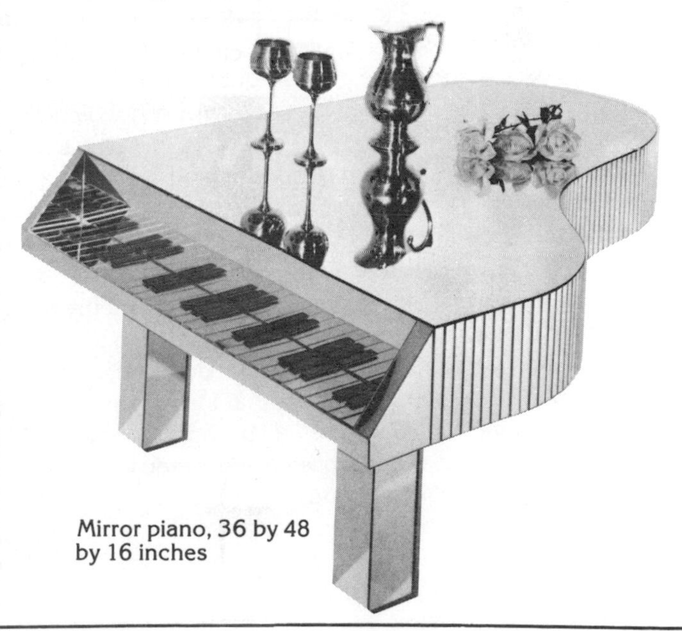

Mirror piano, 36 by 48 by 16 inches

PIANO FOR HIRE

Both Steinway and Baldwin have what is known worldwide as "Concert and Artists" departments, which lend out pianos for concerts held all over the country. Although the pianist only pays for tuning and moving, the latter isn't cheap, considering the piano's size and the union requirement of using five people to move a piano. It costs $325 to send a Steinway from its headquarters to Carnegie Hall—just across the street!

Piano renters are on the run at odd hours. Transporting and servicing pianos for professional dates require skills well beyond the capacity to tune a piano. The moving crew will first put the piano on its side and wrap it in a space blanket to keep climatic changes to a minimum. They then put it in a truck or van, a task which usually requires five or six people. With pianos stored in several locations throughout the country, Pro Piano, a piano rental company, will drive anywhere within an 800-mile radius to deliver a piano for a concert date. Often they will drive all night to deliver a piano. This intensity "adds flavor to our business," says owner Ricard de la Rosa, who started out in the rock music business in San Francisco. "There's a certain outlaw quality to our business," de la Rosa admits. Everyone in the company does everything—they have to drive a truck, be a mechanic, be a piano tuner. You have to break rules, connive, talk people into letting you in when they're not supposed to."

Once the piano arrives at the designated hall, it will be tuned two hours before the concert, although it was tuned before leaving the shop. The artist will naturally test the piano, and the piano rental people must be on hand to make any last-minute changes. "That's where one of the most important aspects of piano technical care comes in," says de la Rosa, "and it's called, very simply, psychology—learning what to do immediately to dissipate fears and anxieties and at the same time to adhere to the problems. Because, after all, I'm talking to people who have spent from thirty to fifty years sitting at the piano, eight hours a day. So when they bring a problem up, the very first thing that I say is, 'Yes, absolutely, you're right.' My priority is the integrity of the piano. I consider myself a slave to the pianist." De la Rosa pinpoints four or five remedies that, although temporary and short-lived, "will burst out and seem like a lot. For example, I might brush the hammers, which has an immediate soothing effect on the tone. Or I may very, very gently needle a hammer, which affects the voicing slightly. The aim is to leave the tone as bombastic as it can be, and yet to conceal that bombasticness. So the pianist is calmed, and the piano is slightly altered. We're being honest, we're just serving all the gods—the music, the artist, the piano, and me."

Many a pianist forms an intense bond with a certain piano, and does not appreciate being separated from that instrument. Classical pianist Gary Graffman developed a thing for "Christine," a "bumptious and brash" piano he met up with in 1963 and nicknamed after a British playgirl then in the news. But "Christine" never replaced the love of Graffman's musical life: a piano identified by the Steinway company as "CD 199." Graffman loved "her enormous bass, her luscious middle register, and her gleaming treble." A rare and generous man, he shared CD 199 with three fellow pianists, and they took turns shipping the piano from concert hall to auditorium to keep up with their frenetic schedules. Finally, they wore out old CD 199, and each pianist went his own way to find a new rented piano he could fall in love with.

One Steinway artist must have shocked the U.S. postal service when she sent a telegram to the company, announcing: I AM DIVORCING NO. 1. SEND ME NO. 2. The pianist, Myra Hess, was talking, of course, about the pianos in her life, and a sudden change of heart.

Every pianist who tours has usually had a share of near catastrophes. The traveling pianist can find him- or herself stranded in some town or hall with a dead-sounding piano—or no instrument at all—regardless of the precautions taken. Sometimes the piano strings break during a performance, or, worse, the piano falls. Bobby Short's piano bench once collapsed under him. Several performers have even had their pianos start to move away from them during performances. (They were playing on pianos placed on wheels that didn't lock in place.)

Like other pianists who tour, André Watts has had his share of piano misfortunes. At one performance, the pedals came off as he was playing. Trying gallantly to hold the pedals up with his feet while he continued to play, Watts finally had to give up and went offstage to bring out the emergency piano technician.

When his piano lid fell off, Malcolm Frager kept right on playing. On the same tour, in South America, the lights went out and Frager also continued to play, by candlelight. On another tour, in the western part of the Soviet Union, a man delivered a letter backstage asking Frager to help him become a spy for the United States.

A near disaster happened to Ruth Laredo in the Midwest. When she arrived on the day of the performance and found an unbelievably bad piano awaiting her, the Baldwin company convinced a tuner-technician to travel 100 miles. "He sat there for hours," she says, "and when people came to the hall they saw this poor guy sitting at the piano. He was a red-bearded Norwegian piano tuner. There were shavings all over. He was doing all kinds of things with the wood to fix the piano. It was a sight to see. He had his undershirt on—it was wild! There were the guts of the piano all over the stage. The orchestra was warming up and he was still tuning the piano. He did a brilliant job—he saved my life!"

Until a pianist is well enough known, he must be continually concerned with the "borrowed friend." José Iturbi used to say, "If you give me a good piano, well, fine, if I play it well. But give me a lousy piano, *then* see what I can do with it." Many pianists do not, however, want that kind of challenge.

Not every pianist playing an abominable piano for hire reacts in such a violent fashion as did the American pianist Myron Kropp during a performance in Bangkok. Reporting on this most unusual concert, the *Los Angeles Times* said that Mr. Kropp suffered a number of technical indignities before he took final action. Kropp had to settle for a piano stool on stage, instead of a bench, and when he began to play the Bach Toccata and Fugue in D-minor, he found that the keys were sticking, including the crucial D in the second octave. Mr. Kropp began to mutter to himself quite audibly from then on. Moving on to other pieces, he found that even more keys were sticking, probably due to the sticky Bangkok climate. Moreover, his stool must have been overgreased, because at one point in the program Kropp found himself turned around, actually facing the audience. People started to laugh, and Kropp was seen kicking the piano instead of operating the pedals. Suddenly, the right front leg of the piano buckled, leaving the entire instrument listing at a 35-degree angle. Soon after, Mr. Kropp jumped off the stage, and the audience assumed that the concert was over and began to applaud. But Mr. Kropp reappeared on stage, carrying a fire ax in his hand. He proceeded to chop at the left leg of the grand piano, which collapsed the weakened legs altogether, and the piano fell with a loud crash. He continued chopping, and had to be restrained by "the ushers . . . with the help of the hotel manager, two Indian watchmen and a passing police corporal, who finally succeeded in disarming Mr. Kropp and dragging him off the stage." Finally, the pianist's ultimate revenge on a piano for hire!

Shopping for a Piano

Your hands may touch many keyboards before you come across the piano that's right for you. Shopping for a piano can be a great adventure and a remarkable way to educate yourself musically.

For most people, buying a piano is a one-time purchasing opportunity. While Liberace has many spectacular antique pianos in his Rare Piano Museum in Las Vegas, and professional pianists often own two instruments, most of us buy one piano as a lifetime investment.

The king of keyboards

Custom-made lucite-and-glass piano

There are many ways to buy a piano, some more obvious than others. You can go through a well-known manufacturer, a dealer who sells several piano makes, or check newspaper ads for private sales and auctions. Pianos sold by individuals are cheaper than those sold by companies. Your piano teacher, piano teacher's tuner, or local music school may also have suggestions. Music stores and music magazines are another good source. Major piano companies sometimes conduct sales, as do large department stores with instrument sections. A great time to buy a piano is at the end of a festival season. Baldwin sells "Tanglewood pianos"—those that have been used for performance and rehearsal—at much lower prices. You might play the same piano that was played by Misha Dichter or André Watts!

To educate yourself about the different types of new and used pianos, visit dealers and showrooms and try out the instruments. Don't be intimidated—you're going to have to live with your purchase for a long time. It is a good idea to bring music along with you to play on different models. Keep in mind that a piano will sound different according to the room's acoustics. In a large, empty showroom it will sound brighter and louder. The sound will be more mellow and softer if you have carpets or drapes. Talk to piano salespeople, and ask for brochures.

Finding a reputable dealer is an essential factor that most piano buyers don't think about, according to Baldwin salespeople. Confident dealers will appreciate your needs and aims in piano shopping, and give you honest opinions of the pianos they have on hand. The quality of the dealer's piano service department is an important postpurchase factor as well.

A classic reference book in this area is *The Piano Owner's Guide: How to Buy and Care for a Piano*, by Carl D. Schmeckel (Scribner's). The National Piano Manufacturer's Association, at 230 North Michigan Avenue in Chicago, also publishes an informative pamphlet, "The Consumer's Guide to Buying a Piano," which it updates periodically.

Once you've spotted a piano, especially if it is a secondhand instrument, take a technician with you to inspect it. Even if you are a pianist yourself, you may not be able to spot flaws in the instrument that a technician would normally look for. A technician will not only meticulously inspect the instrument's action, pin block, sounding board, and metal plate, but also will guarantee the stability and integrity of the piano's structure. A technician will tell you if the piano needs any repairs, and will give you an estimate or an appraisal. An estimate is simply a summing up of how much the piano is presently worth and of how much it would cost you to fix it. An appraisal is an overall analysis of how good the piano is, and how much is required to put it into good condition. Usually the technician charges a fee of $40 to $50 and takes about a half hour, but it will be well worth it. You can find a competent technician through the Piano Technicians Guild. Otherwise, consult the Yellow Pages or ask for a referral. If a technician can't be found, consider taking along your piano teacher or a musician friend who may be able to advise you about the tonal quality and action.

Piano prices range from a few hundred dollars for a rudimentary spinet to well over $10,000 for a medium grand piano. Some piano costs for 1983 are as follows: A small brand-name upright costs about $1200; a large upright (studio piano) about $1800; and grand pianos start at about $3000 and go all the way up to $30,000 for a performer's concert grand.

Piano dealers agree that people usually work their way up to a superior instrument. A beginner may be happy with a $400 Wadsworth spinet while discovering how serious his interest in music is. Piano experts, though, will advise prospective owners to buy the best. The rule of thumb is, the better the piano, the longer its life. One other piano-shopping rule to think about: the bigger the piano, the better the tone.

One last bit of advice: When you're finding out what conditions accompany the piano you're buying, do make sure it's a company-insured piano. If not, insure it. Constance Keene, head of the piano faculty at the Manhattan School of Music, relates one student's unforgettable piano lesson: "She was having her uninsured piano hoisted through her window, and it fell."

English Bentside spinet

PIANO SHOPPING CHECKLIST

When it comes to buying a piano, even professional pianists are often uncertain about what to look for and listen to. The following checklist offers suggestions, hints, and questions to ask before you buy.

The Workings of the Piano

KEYS. A piano should have a full-size eighty-eight-note keyboard.

Are all eighty-eight keys in place?

Are there fifty-two white and thirty-six black keys?

Do any keys stick?

Do all the keys rise to the right height?

STRINGS. A piano should have a full set of about 230 strings: one or two copper-wound strings for each of the lower (bass) notes, and three plain wire strings for each of the higher (treble) notes. To check the strings, open up the piano lid and take a look. (For uprights, it's the bottom door that opens.)

Are at least 230 strings present and accounted for?

Are they in perfect condition (unbroken, perfectly strung)?

HAMMERS. Make sure the felts on the hammers are not worn.

SOUNDING BOARD. The size and quality of the sounding board are very important if a piano is to have a good tone and volume. The sounding board runs the length of the metal plate, which holds the strings.

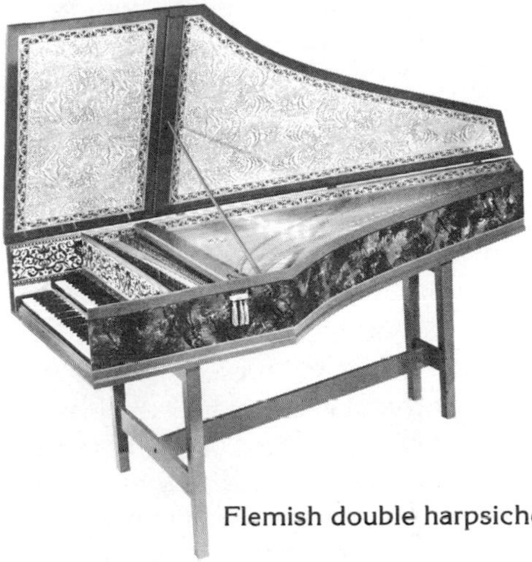

Flemish double harpsichord

Early nineteenth century American pianoforte

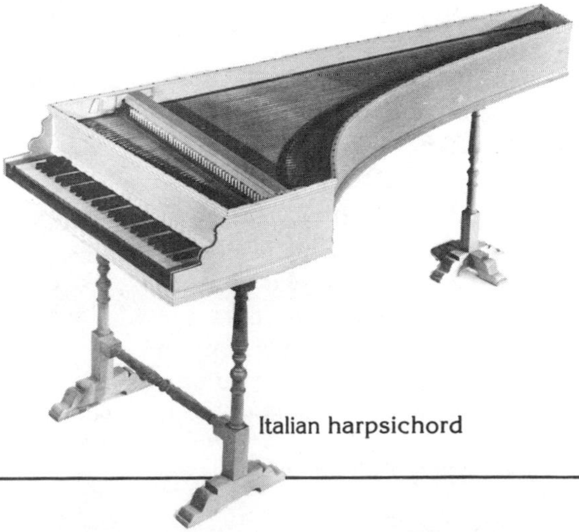

Italian harpsichord

Make sure the sounding board has no cracks.

See that the bridges, which connect the strings with the sounding board, are not cracked or split.

THE ACTION. This is the most complicated part of the piano's mechanism, and should be checked carefully by a technician.

Play the notes up and down the keyboard. Is there evenness in tone? Does the piano respond?

PEDALS. Most pianos have three pedals, though some may have only two. The right pedal is the sustaining pedal—it makes the notes last longer. The left pedal is the soft pedal, for softer sounds or special effects. The center pedal (if there is one) is the sostenuto pedal—it sustains one or more isolated tones. Advanced pianists need all three pedals. Basically, a beginner needs only the sustaining pedal. But give yourself the option of three pedals, if possible.

GENERAL INSPECTION. Make sure the piano's inner workings are clean and rust-free. Inspect for chips, breaks, or anything unusual. If you hear anything rattle, watch out: the piano's in trouble.

The Piano Case or Cabinet

An attractive-looking piano is, of course, desirable. But keep in mind that an expensive-looking finish or cabinet style with a poorly constructed musical instrument inside will probably not serve your best interests. The best-looking, more expensive wood finishes are walnut and mahogany (or rosewood, if you can find it). Other popular finishes include cherry, oak, ebony, and Formica. The different styles of piano cases are contemporary, classic, French provincial, Early American, American traditional, Italian provincial, or custom-made.

Examine the wood for luster and touch. Is the wood unblemished? Is it smooth to the touch?

Look at the music rack and leg design. It will help you to determine whether the cabinet style will be compatible with your home decor.

Do you want a piano bench or a stool? A regular duet bench can cost you anywhere from $150 to $400, and comes with a music compartment. This is the most popular, practical, and aesthetically pleasing piece to have. A swivel-top piano stool or chair runs around $125. It will adjust to your height, but it isn't as sturdy or long-lasting as a bench. An artist's concert bench—the adjustable kind on which you turn the side handles—runs between $300 and $400, and is made for the individual pianist. Many nonperformers use it, as it is the most durable piano bench.

Make sure the piano comes complete with a suitable piano bench or stool. Try out different benches or stools for size, comfort and solidity.

The Sound of the Piano

The sound is the most important element in the piano.

Ask for a demonstration of several pianos of the same type and size. No two pianos of even the same model are the same.

In a good piano, the low notes sound deep and resonant, and the high notes sound clear, but not harsh. The piano should have an even tone throughout.

Keep listening. Be discerning. Trust your ear or your expert's.

If you're a nonplayer, don't be seduced by a loud, brassy tone which may bore or tire you over time, or by a dull, quiet tone which may irritate you.

Technical questions for the expert or for the salesperson:

Will the piano tune well?

How long will it hold its pitch?

Are the sounding board, joints, and pin block made with first-rate materials?

In what condition are the cast-iron frame and backposts?

How solid is the back frame?

How solid is the piano's construction overall?

Are the legs strong?

What kinds of wood have been used where?

How durable is the piano?

Special Considerations

These finer points may not occur to you in the heat of the shopping experience, and can run you into money and headaches.

MOVING A PIANO. Are moving charges included in the purchase price? Usually the piano dealer's initial price does include moving the piano to your home. Use a professional piano mover—experience counts when moving such a delicate, heavy object.

Will the piano fit through your door? When you're measuring it, also measure the stairs or elevator. One brand-new pianist had windows with unmovable heavy bars across them, preventing pianos as well as thieves

A New Orleans piano auction of the 1940s

from entering. He had to find a piano that would fit through his door, so he bought a trim little Winter spinet.

Can the piano be hoisted through a window? You don't want to have to take part of the building apart to get the piano inside—which has been done on occasion, when a window was too narrow.

INSURANCE. Is the piano company insured? Perhaps your piano dealer can offer you special piano insurance.

You may want to increase your household insurance to cover the piano. Theft isn't that likely, considering the instrument's bulk, but you should be protected against fires, floods, and other damage.

Is there a warranty? Some new brand-name pianos carry a five-to-ten-year warranty that may or may not include an initial tuning, another tuning six months later, and one regulation for the action.

"Sonata for Piano and Dog"

Where You Can Buy a Piano.

The best known, most reliable acoustic piano manufacturers in the United States are listed below, with addresses and telephone numbers of their main offices.

Aeolian Pianos, Inc. 2718 Pershing Avenue, Memphis, TN 38112. (901) 324-7351.

Baldwin Piano & Organ Company. 1801 Gilbert Avenue, Cincinnati, OH 45202. (513) 852-7000.

Bösendorfer Pianos. C/O Kimball Piano & Organ Company, 1549 Royal Street, Jasper, IN 47546. (812) 482-1600.

Everett Piano Company. 900 Indiana Avenue, South Haven, MI 49090. (800) 253-3146.

Kawai. C/O Kawai America Corporation, 24200 South Vermont Avenue, Harbor City, CA 90710. (213) 534-2350.

Sohmer & Company. Main Street, Ivoryton, CT 06442. (203) 767-2675.

Steinway & Sons. Steinway Place, Long Island City, NY 11105. (212) 721-2600.

Wurlitzer. The Music People, DeKalb, IL 60115. (815) 756-2771.

Yamaha Pianos. Yamaha International Corporation, 6600 Orangethorpe Avenue, Buena Park, CA 90620. (714) 522-9011.

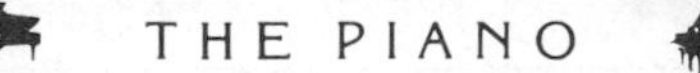

UNUSUAL PIANO SHAPES AND USES

The first typewriters had piano-style keyboards and were the size of kitchen tables. Even today's modern electric typewriter as well as the word processor and computer can ultimately trace their ancestry to the piano keyboard.

● In the 1860s, an American inventory registered a patent for a piano bed; another variation on the traditional piano was one built for players without arms.

● Piano merchant and publisher Bob Pierce is so crazy about the piano that he has a desk in the shape of a grand piano, a grand piano—shape pipe, and an enormous collection of piano miniatures and decals.

● People have been known to use the space beneath their piano for:

Storing firewood in crowded apartments

Safekeeping Italian pottery and crystal glasses

Lovemaking

Setting rabbit and hamster cages

Keeping their Apple computer terminals.

Taking Care of the Piano

A piano has 12,000 parts, a standard American car only 14,000—and a piano doesn't have to take you anywhere! Yet car owners who rush their motorized instruments in for repairs, brake adjustments, or tuning will assume that pianos can somehow take care of themselves and will leave them sitting in corners for months or even years at a time, hugging the radiator, exposed to the sun, or collecting dust, like some great hulking pieces of furniture. Despite their imposing size and appearance, pianos are extremely sensitive musical instruments that are affected by any atmospheric change or condition, including dampness, dryness, heat, and cold. Pianos will go out of tune even if you don't play them.

Piano tuners are usually the first people called in on a piano-care case. Piano technicians, mechanics who do physical repairs and reconditioning, can also be tuners, and vice versa. (In Japan, every tuner has to be able to also do all the technical work.) Technicians will string the piano, fix broken keys, and repair the sounding board, the bridge, or any structural part. They also regulate the piano for an even response, and install, build, adjust, or time the action, the mechanical equipment which causes the piano strings to vibrate from the pressure of the pianist's fingers. Tuning and voicing the piano are the next critical steps. Masaro Tsumita, a Steinway master technician, stresses the importance of voicing: "The hammer has to hit the strings *exactly* at the same place. One note may be mellow, another harsh or metallic." The voicing tool used by the technician separates and loosens the interlocking wood fibers to produce a warmer, mellower sound.

Restoration of antique pianos requires knowledge of wood, so it is not surprising that many restorers are also cabinetmakers. These specialists are magicians who can make an old piano sound and look better than new: they rebuild it on the inside, refinish it on the outside. At Beethoven Piano Movers, Carl Demsler rebuilds as well as moves fine old pianos. He warns that he never puts new parts, such as sounding boards, into very old instruments since it changes the sound completely. Demsler had recently taken a Steinway "B" from the 1920s and polished the case—applying fifteen coats of walnut stain to make it look practically new.

Kalman Detrich, who rebuilds and restores antique pianos, has instruments ranging from early nineteenth-century models to supermodern lucite-and-glass

Restored piano

novelty and "Hollywood" pianos chosen for use in films, such as the piano that was dropped from a window in the movie *The World According to Garp*. Detrich feels that pianists should know more about how pianos are built so that they can control the sound. Accordingly, technicians are revealing secrets of the trade that formerly died with master craftsmen. "How many teachers tell you that the tone will somehow come out round (full, with depth) because of the way your finger goes down on the key?" he asks. "Actually, before you reach the bottom of the key you've lost control over the tone. I wonder how anybody can spend six hours a day at the piano, every day, and not know this." His recommendation: "Every music college should have at least a one-semester course on how the piano works for those who are going to spend the rest of their lives in front of it."

Courses in piano construction and tuning are being offered more widely for adventurous pianists at schools such as UCLA, the New School in New York City, and the New England Conservatory of Music in Boston. Ambitious people are even building their own instruments with precut pieces in kits—modern reconstruction of eighteenth-century and nineteenth-century fortepianos based upon simpler models rather than on the 12,000-part modern piano with its steel frame. These homemade instruments are easier to construct than it might seem, although they can't produce the same rich, complex tones of manufactured instruments. The most popular do-it-yourself keyboard instruments are harpsichords, clavichords, and fortepianos, which enable you to play Bach, Vivaldi, Mozart, and early Beethoven on the instruments the composers wrote for. One leading keyboard manufacturer is Zuckermann Harpsichords, which sells both kits and finished instruments. A simple clavichord costs $470 to build ($975 to buy completed), and takes twenty-five to forty hours to put together. An Italian harpsichord, of moderate complexity, costs $1675 for the kit, $3760 already built, and takes 80 to 120 hours to build. A Flemish double-manual harpsichord, one of the most developed instruments, costs $2560 to make in 120 to 240 hours; a finished harpsichord costs $7190; a fortepiano costs $3155 to build, $8155 to buy, and takes 300 to 500 hours to make.

A Zuckermann fortepiano built from a kit

ASK THE PIANO LADY

In this section the Piano Lady shares the many piano secrets she's discovered over the years.

Q: I'm about to buy my first piano. Where is the ideal place for it?
Piano Lady: **Bringing a piano into your home is like welcoming a newborn baby: your life, as well as your living space, will never be the same. Your living arrangements may have to change drastically. This could be your opportunity to redecorate—and people have also moved for less!**

Do not put your piano near a radiator, fireplace, air duct, a window that's usually open, or in a direct draft. Ideally, you should keep a piano room in the low 70s for temperature, with forty-five to fifty percent humidity. Pianos should be put against an inside wall, although an outside wall will do if it's fairly well-insulated.

"I've gone into a home and found a grand piano sitting right next to a French door that's open, with the dampness and dryness coming in," laments John Steinway, who ought to know about proper piano care. He protests further, "Or, the piano's next to a big main heating outlet or an air conditioner. The poor piano is just sitting there, exposed to all of this, subjected to changes in humidity, temperature, heat and cold. You wouldn't want to stand there all day in front of all that. Well, the piano doesn't either!"

Man and Woman, 1910, by Harrison Fisher

Q: How often should I have my piano tuned and regulated?

Piano Lady: **Baldwin master technician Joe Vitti, who tunes at Tanglewood, says a piano should ideally be tuned four times a year, at every change of season, or at least twice a year. John Steinway recommends that a piano be tuned two or three times a year with the changes of season, and four times if possible, even if it isn't played a great deal. "It protects the investment," he explains. If the piano is heavily used, then you'll have to decide what's necessary. For example, a piano that's played every day in a recording studio or in a live performance should be tuned daily.**

Also, a piano that is played a lot should be re-regulated every three or four years, depending on usage. Regulating a piano involves adjusting and timing the piano's action. Pianos can go out of regulation due to normal wear, shrinkage or expansion of the wooden parts due to climatic conditions, damage from moths or mice, et cetera. That's why it's wise to "spot regulate" to keep the piano machinery operating at its best level all the time, and to re-regulate every few years so that the keyboard, hammer action and damper-action assemblies are in fine form. "It's like car maintenance," Steinway explains. "You can't run a machine and expect it to run forever—and the piano is a machine as well as a musical instrument."

Q: How do I clean the piano keys? Do they sell a special product in piano stores?
Piano Lady: There are lots of practical solutions as well as old wives' tales that people have come up with over the years for cleaning piano keys. Except for dabbing warm milk on the ivories, probably any of them will work. Milk makes the keys smell, and coats them with a sticky substance. Some pianists swear by soap and water, others by seltzer water. The National Piano Manufacturers Association recommends washing the black and white notes separately because the black finish can rub off on the cloth. Ricard de la Rosa of Pro Piano suggests using Windex—the liquid kind, which has a light solution of ammonia. "We find it's the very best thing—just spray it on the keys and wipe it right off with a paper towel." A popular cleaning solution among piano technicians is two tablespoons of vinegar mixed with one gallon of warm water. But watch out! Don't let any liquid or dampness get on the strings. They're made of steel and will rust. Be sure to dry the keys thoroughly after cleaning to prevent dampness and to give them that nicely polished glow. You may even come up with your own cleaning solution. No matter what you use, treat those keys with tender loving care and use something soft—a cloth, cheesecloth, or, best of all, a diaper!
Q: Is it all right to use furniture polish on the outside of a piano?
Piano Lady: Certain piano manuals will warn you to stay away from polish, recommending instead that you dampen a clean cloth with water to remove finger marks, grease stains, and dust. Find out whether your piano case is wood, lacquer, varnish, or polyester from the sales manager or the person you bought it from. Each piano company gives its own advice on care for the case. Steinway recommends clear lacquer for their piano cases. Ricard de la Rosa feels that furniture paste wax and coatings are admissible. Pianos with a high-polish finish—such as a Yamaha or a Hamburg Steinway—require different care. For a high-luster synthetic piano, de la Rosa says, polish would become a grimy, lumpy mess when applied to a nonwood surface. What he recommends is a little bit of lighter fluid or paint thinner applied with a light cotton cloth. Just rub in the direction of the grain or finish. And if you don't know what kind of case you've got, use something mild, such as lemon oil polish.

Q: How often do you need to clean the inside of the piano?
Piano Lady: A piano should be thoroughly cleaned every two to three years. Dirt and debris falling onto the strings and settling on the soundboard deaden the tone and can eventually interfere with the finely fitted parts. Pianos, even small uprights, are relatively large pieces of furniture and can collect a lot of dust and dirt. Grand pianos are especially dirt-prone, particularly on the soundboard. That's one reason for keeping the piano lid closed when the piano's not in use.

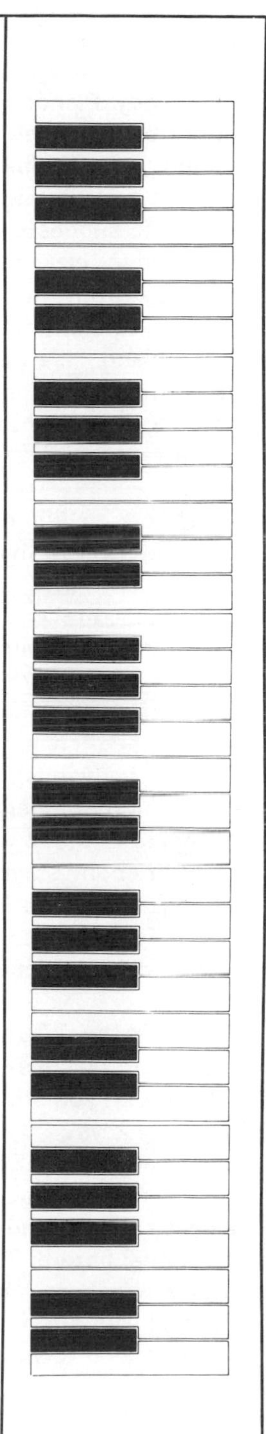

Q: What about using my blow dryer to clean the inside of my piano?
Piano Lady: Pianos don't like having hot air blown directly onto their strings. John Steinway knows of an ingenious way to clean the inside of a piano. He suggests taking the hose of a vacuum cleaner, putting it on the other end from the way you'd usually vacuum, and blowing everything *out* of the piano. "It's much easier to vacuum the room than to try to get inside a piano and bang the dirt out with a vacuum cleaner," he says.

Q: Is there anything I can do about the scratches on the outside of my piano?
Piano Lady: I recently heard of a curious way to fix scratches, and it seems to work perfectly. Take the meat from natural walnuts and rub it over the scratches, filling in all indentations. Use varnish to match the color. Another ingenious piano secret I've heard is that if you can't get ahold of ebony stain, use black or mahogany ink or a Magic Marker. This is for temporary repair, but dries very quickly and looks fine.

Q: What's the difference between ivories and plastics? Which one is better? Can you still buy a piano that has ivory keys?
Piano Lady: When ivories get old, they turn yellow and crack, cutting the pianist's fingers and creating an occupational hazard. Their aging process is relentless, and cannot be stopped with ammonia or soap. Sometimes a technician will replace them with plastics. What makes ivories so good? Pianists say they have a wonderful touch, a great rapport with the fingertips. Plastic keys, they find, are smooth and don't absorb sweat as well, and your fingers can slide. Since endangered species legislation was passed to protect elephants, it is now illegal to manufacture pianos with ivory keys in the United States. American piano manufacturers have completely switched to plastic keys, but some of the European pianos, such as the Bösendorfer, are still made with ivory. In the end, pianists say, it doesn't matter what the keys are made of, just how the music is made.

Woman at the Piano, circa 1917, by Elie Nadelman

Q: What do I do about sticky keys? And how do I prevent them from sticking?

Piano Lady: **Sticky keys are the most common complaint of piano owners. There are five common causes for sticky keys: warped piano parts, foreign objects inside the piano, key bushings—the lining that reduces friction as the keys move—that are too tight, one key interfering with the one next to it, and misalignment of the keys. You might solve the whole problem by looking into the piano carefully with a flashlight. If you see that something has fallen into the piano that's not supposed to be there and you can remove it gently by yourself, then you're in luck. If it's only the white keys that are sticking, then your keyslip, the wood strip that runs the length of the keybed and protects the keys, may be warped. For both grand and upright pianos, simply insert a matchbook, business card, or a small piece of cardboard between the keyslip and keyblock at each end of the keyboard. A small piece of cardboard placed like this is called a shim. Shims create clearance between the keyslip and the key front and will often solve the problem. If not, don't panic. Call a reliable piano tuner for advice. He or she may tell you how to go ahead with your mechanical investigation if you trust your ability not to damage the piano.**

Q: Can I do any piano repair myself? It's so costly and inconvenient to call for a technician every time my A sounds sharp or I notice any little problem.

Piano Lady: **Yes and no! You *can* learn certain procedures and some basics in tuning. Many performing pianists are now taking the trouble to learn the rudiments, and quite a few music schools and extension courses now offer piano tuning and repair courses. A piano tuned by a trained technician, rather than by a beginner, will usually sound better and last longer, but an amateur tuning can correct horrible problems, at least temporarily. Pianists who learn to do some tuning and make minor repairs have been known to save their own skins during a performance. If you want to be ready to repair on occasion, my advice is to learn a few piano repair skills from an expert.**

Q: Do you recommend a humidifier to give the piano added moisture?

Piano Lady: **Many pianists use humidifiers in the winter and dehumidifiers in the summer to provide just the right amount of moisture needed to protect the piano. These items can be fitted to the instrument, either placed inside an upright piano or attached underneath a grand piano. Some people who live in areas of drastic climate changes use what is called a climate-control system to protect the piano from all harsh climatic effects.**

Marta Istomin, a cellist who was the wife of Pablo Casals, cared for their piano in Puerto Rico, so she always used a dehumidifier as well as air conditioning to fight the tropical dampness and heat. Technician

Lucas Mason says he greatly prefers natural humidity in the room. For a dry New York apartment, for example, he advises people to buy pretty bowls and fill them with a few colorful rocks and water. That way the water evaporates into the air and becomes a cohesive part of the room. Instead of settling on the strings, the water creates a mist on the piano.

One imaginative pianist, the musical director of a summer camp in the Adirondack Mountains, fearing for her piano's condition during the cold, damp summer nights, daringly had a 40-watt electric bulb installed right into the piano. She'd keep the light on in the evening before her shows to keep the piano warm and toasty, and would shut it off at night. Because of the fire hazard, I wouldn't go so far as to recommend this method.

Q: My landlord is making my life miserable. He only wants me to practice during the day, when he's not home. Sometimes I *must* practice late at night. What can I do besides moving into a private home?

Piano Lady: If you live in an apartment house, there are no legal restrictions about practice time in most cities, unless there's a restriction about pianists as tenants in the lease. Like dogs and children, pianists are sometimes considered "undesirable" and are not allowed to move in. If you want to maintain friendly relations with the people surrounding you, you might want to take it upon yourself, especially if you're a professional pianist who *must* practice much of the time, to do what full-time pianists have felt obliged to do: improve or soundproof your practice studio. Concert pianist Emanuel Ax followed some simple acoustical

Angry harpsichordist and ensemble

rules with successful results: he inserted three-inch-thick rubber blocks containing protruding steel rods under and into the piano legs to deaden the sound. Misha Dichter, on the other hand, had to spend considerable time and money to quiet the sound—and his neighbor. Dichter rebuilt his entire studio, costing him the equivalent, he says, of a house, and ended up by building a room within a room. A new floor was superimposed on the existing carpet, the walls were padded, and thick oak bookcases were placed against the walls. The sound that resulted was ultradry and muted, like that in a hushed museum. Now, Dichter says, anyplace else he plays seems flattering. Most pianists don't have to go to such extremes as did Dichter or Marcel Proust, who had his entire apartment lined in cork. Sometimes simple adjustments such as putting a carpet on the floor, hanging a rug from a wall, or installing a bookcase will muffle the sound sufficiently.

Q: Is it all right to move a piano on rollers?
Piano Lady: Yes, but don't rely just on the rollers—you risk breaking a leg (the piano's, not your own). You'll need three people, one at each corner, to move a grand, and two people for an upright. Lift the piano slightly as you roll it. But if you're going any distance, you might want to call in a professional piano mover, called a "humper," who does this every day. Their trucks make moving a piano a relative breeze.

Q: My front door is too narrow to fit the piano I have my heart set on—can the legs be taken off? I'm distraught.
Piano Lady: The piano legs are often removed when a piano's being moved. They can be screwed on or off in three minutes' time. It's easy.

Piano movers in India

Q: I live in a fourth-floor walkup with a narrow staircase. What do I do?
Piano Lady: There may be a better route. Your piano will probably slip right in through your window, if the window is a standard size. Hire a hoister—and get insurance. Hoisting, also known as rigging, costs $300 minimum for one flight, and slightly more for each flight thereafter. This is a delicate procedure and represents two to three hours of work.

Q: I've heard that you can't play the piano if you have small hands. Is this true?
Piano Lady: There are a number of great concert pianists who have small hands. Alicia de Larrocha, for instance, is an internationally acclaimed Spanish pianist whose hands span hardly more than an octave. Large hands are another problem—pianists find that they can get in the way at times. You can play the piano no matter how big or little your fingers are, or how great your hand span is. Trying to stretch out your fingers is an obsession some pianists have had. Robert Schumann devised a contraption that attached to the wall, from which he would hang his fourth and fifth fingers at night. He stretched them out until he ruined them.

Q: I've read that Glenn Gould always used to soak his hands in hot water for twenty minutes before a performance. Is this a kooky idea or a good tip?
Piano Lady: It's true that some pianists, such as Gould, have sworn by this ritual. Soaking your hands in hot water before playing seems to stimulate flexibility and circulation. Other pianists soak their hands in cold water to wake up the nerves. Just shaking your hands vigorously will rid them of stored-up tension.

A rooftop delivery

Alicia de Larrocha

The dangling piano

Piano Tuners are grand and upright people

THE PIANO TUNER'S TALE

Piano tuners may be the best known piano craftspeople, but what they actually do to your piano—and how—seems mysterious. Piano tuner Jean Newton reminisces, "I used to think that piano tuners were strange old Italian men who did unmentionable things to the piano."

A tuner's first order is to correct the unisons of the strings so that the proper pitch (the high-low sound of a musical tone) will result when any one of the eighty-eight notes is sounded. These notes correspond not to one, but to two or three strings, which have to vibrate in perfect unison. These unisons are the first thing a tuner's ear will pick up.

After setting the pitch, the tuner is concerned with what is called "equal temperament," a process of adjusting the number of string vibrations of each note to an exact relationship with the same factors of all 230-odd strings.

The physical act of tuning the piano—turning the hitchpins, which hook the strings—requires tremendous strength. The tension of all the strings equals eighteen to twenty tons and is capable of powering a hoist which could lift forty or more heavy old uprights simultaneously. Also, it's important to hold the tuning hammer correctly and to angle it snugly down on, but not to bend, the pins—all of which takes practice, patience, and a great love of hanging around pianos. It took Jean Newton two years to develop the necessary back and shoulder muscle endurance to be able to tune a piano and not feel the strain. She says, though, that any woman can develop her body to do this, and that "If women can be policemen as well as concert pianists, with all the strength that takes, they can certainly be piano technicians!"

The Yellow Pages are filled with the names of tuners, but, as with other skilled craftsmen, it's hard to find a good one. To tune well requires a knowledge of acoustics and piano theory along with a highly developed ear, which is different in some ways from a musical ear: You have to hear tone quality, not just accurate pitch. "In Western music the natural ratios are all out of tune to a small degree, because of the overtones," tuner-teacher Lucas Mason explains. "The piano has a lot of weird sounds in it; all pianos do. No matter how good your mathematical calculations, you have to make adjustments. That's why a machine can't do what the human ear can. Tuning *is* a scientific process, but must, in the end, be checked by the ear. Machines are more accurate than the average good ear," Mason continues, "but they don't tune according to the sound of the note."

Piano tuning is certainly not dull. Tuners perform their services wherever there are pianos—on boats and in lofts, in barns and mansions, and even, in Paris, in the

MUSICAL WONDERS

There are more blind piano tuners than you'd imagine. Of the 3000 piano tuners registered in the Piano Technicians Guild, 75 are blind. The common explanation is that people without sight are more sensitive to sound, but there's a more practical reason: piano tuning was one of the first professions open to blind people. Tuners need to rely for accuracy not only on their ears but also on their feel for physical vibrations.

Louis Braille, an organist, originally invented Braille as a way for blind people to read music.

Deaf people can tune pianos, as well as lutes, viols, spinets, or any other stringed instruments, as long as they understand the physics of sound. The sound made by a vibrating string depends on its length, its mass, and how much it is stretched.

subway (concerts are now given in the Métro). Piano owners, assuming that they are being helpful, will offer tuners strange appliances such as wrenches, rolling pins, and hair dryers. Tuners also come across peculiar pianos—ones with strings underneath, or with two sets of strings. Tuners and their clients have an immediate mutual point of interest, which enables the customer to trust the tuner, and sometimes to even feel a sense of intimacy—propositions of all kinds are made to tuners. It's evidently a common occurrence, for example, for tuners to arrive at someone's home and find not merely an available piano, but also a naked woman—or man—awaiting them. Scot Lockhart, who calls himself "the Happy Tuner" to set himself apart from tuners he's found to be unfriendly or hermitlike, has encountered quite a few of these situations and says that a tuner's life is like a milkman's. Once, when Lockhart was hard at work, the lady of the house left him alone. When the phone rang, he answered it. "It was her husband. He was angry. I quickly tuned the piano and got out of there fast." Often, he says, tuners are subjected to overfriendly animals. He once had to tune a piano with a cat sitting on his head.

On another occasion he was called in to clean a piano in a penthouse apartment on Central Park West. "I examined this new, custom-made piano and told the man it was the cleanest piano I had ever seen. 'It's dirty!' he shouted. The apartment itself was huge and almost devoid of other furniture. The man had laid Saran Wrap on the floor beneath the piano. He left the room, and one or two minutes later I said, 'It's clean now.' 'Good,' he said. He gave me $30 and I left. I guess that was my first exorcism."

Perhaps the tuner who calibrates your piano regulates your own inner harmonies and vibrations at the same time. Tuner Lucas Mason agrees: "People get very personal about their pianos. I have people who feel that the "laying on of hands" cures their piano. I've received letters from people saying, 'I came home today after you tuned the piano, and it was just smiling at me.' They really get the feeling that you're performing a ritual, that your good soul carries over into the piano, and the music feels better after that. Piano tuning is almost mystical for some people."

Music Lesson by Henri Matisse

Fats Waller

2

THE PIANIST

Franz Liszt and admiring audience

The Making of a Pianist

Many pianist watchers are convinced that an early start is the way to the pianists' pantheon. The French newsweekly *Le Point* concurred in a recent article, stating that there is a timetable for a hopeful virtuoso interested in having a solo career. According to the article, the crucial checkpoints are these: The pianist plays his first scales at age four, enters a conservatory by twelve, and wins a few international prizes before twenty. Recordings come next, followed, of course, by tours abroad. And if the pianist is still under thirty, that fateful age, the future looks quite promising.

Several contemporary pianists share similar stories about how and why they began to play. "I went to the piano and played *God Bless America* at age two, and no one had taught me," classical pianist Ruth Laredo remembers. "It's not so amazing," she adds. "Children talk when they're two—little kids pick things up."

What drew classical artist Jorge Bolet to the piano? "I'm sure that on the day I was born, at seven o'clock in the morning, I heard the piano," he says. "My sister was very talented and she practiced a great deal. I'm sure she practiced that day and every other day after that." His parents and siblings have told Bolet that even before he was one year old, "whenever my sister started practicing or playing, I would set up the biggest howl in the world. The only way to quiet me was to take me and put me right beside the piano, where I'd lie in my crib for hours, completely quiet, as long as she was playing." When he was four and a half, his sister took him to his first recital, to hear pianist Rudolf Ganz at the National Theatre in Havana. "I saw a man up on the stage and decided at that moment that that's where I wanted to be, and that was what I wanted to be. I decided then and there to be a concert pianist, and I have never deviated from that course."

A child prodigy, Artur Rubinstein sang constantly for the first few years of his life, but refused to speak. When his parents bought an upright piano so that his older sisters could take lessons, he "was so overwhelmed by the appearance of this divine instrument that from then on the drawing room became my paradise. Yelling and crying being my only defenses, I employed these weapons freely when anyone attempted to remove me from there."

It wasn't until the age of forty-seven, however, that Rubinstein's career began in earnest. His early tour of America had not met with great success, and in Berlin,

Marian McPartland

Jorge Bolet

Misha and Cipa Dichter

penniless and disappointed with his life, he had tried to kill himself at age twenty. When the effort failed, he was almost literally born again. "Was it to be said of me that I *could* have been a great pianist? Was this the kind of legacy to leave to my wife and children?" Not at all, Rubinstein decided, and he went on to do a vast series of concerts, tours, and recordings, including ten Carnegie Hall concerts within two weeks at the age of seventy-one. When Rubinstein died in 1983, he was considered one of the greatest pianists of the century.

Jazz pianist Marian McPartland heard her mother play Chopin and other romantic composers; it sounded good to her, and she decided to try it. "All I remember is climbing up on the stool, putting cushions on it, and just playing, probably not very well at first. I played for the kids at school, and I learned all those nursery rhymes, and anything I could hear sung or played. My parents steered away from giving me lessons—I never had any till I was seventeen. But that was it—the piano was for me."

Brazilian-born Cipa Dichter, duo pianist and wife of concert pianist Misha Dichter, made her debut at age sixteen with Brazil's symphony orchestra. She, too, started playing at a tender age, and claims: "I can't remember life without the piano. I remember speaking, walking, talking, and playing the piano—it was always one of my senses." At one point, Cipa wanted to be a dancer, but her father wouldn't allow it. "The piano was my chance for theatricality."

Lorin Hollander

Bob James

Liberace was a child prodigy who "had a love for the piano that began when I was four years old. I played by ear, first of all." Famous Polish pianist Ignaz Jan Paderewski, a family friend, convinced Liberace's parents to begin his musical training early. "I was fortunate to get a scholarship when I was seven—to the Wisconsin College of Music—and it lasted for seventeen years!"

Popular composer-pianist Bob James, who writes the music for TV's *Taxi*, began to sit in on his sister's piano lessons when he was four, "anxious, waiting, and eager." "In Marshall, Missouri, I was considered a prodigy," says James modestly. "There weren't that many pianists there, so I stood out. If I had grown up in New York City I don't know if they would have considered me a prodigy." Finally, a teacher tested him when he was five years old, found that he had perfect pitch, and recommended to his mother that he start lessons right away. "I considered myself very lucky to have started young because at age eight, nine, or ten it's hard to put in that time for the rudimentary things you have to learn at the piano," James says. Many musicians also feel that starting the piano very early, as most of these pianists did, is crucial, if not critical, because the child can develop and stretch his muscles at the keyboard before his body has developed fully.

Rock 'n' roll player-composer Jan Hammer (formerly with the Jeff Beck Group and Mahavishnu) is now known worldwide as a synthesizer player, but developed as an acoustic piano player. The son of two Czechoslovakian musicians, at the age of four Jan was playing by reproducing sounds he heard and writing his own tunes.

Later, he became attracted to drums because they were fun to play, but it was at the piano where Jan developed his musical ear and compositional skills. He admits: "I played the piano for my parents, the drums for myself. At times I even felt threatened by the piano, which sometimes looks like it's got teeth, so all you see if you're a little kid is this big mouth with teeth staring at you."

Now the keyboard player for the rock group Kid Creole and the Coconuts, Peter Schott heard his grandmother play when he was four or five. He felt terribly attracted to the sound, but "it really made me mad that I couldn't just sit down and do it. That's what drives you to study and to practice ten hours a day, which I did later on."

Classical pianist Lorin Hollander became involved in music when he was two years old. He knew all the notes, had perfect pitch, and had begun to compose. At three he was playing the piano, at four and five memorizing the works of Bach, Mozart, and Schubert and starting to concertize. "I was playing concerts at six and made my debut in Carnegie Hall when I was eleven, although I had played with the orchestra prior to that, when I was ten."

Jan Hammer

Peter Schott

Contemporary keyboard player (with the Who) Tim Gorman was recognized to be a child prodigy and carted off to a Belgian piano teacher, and was called on to play for people all the time. He resented being separated from the other kids because of his talent, and also having to perform for people when so young—"Now, ma?" he would ask his mother. He wasn't even allowed to play sports, to protect his hands. But today, at thirty, Tim is grateful for those piano lessons.

Plenty of careers have happened in other ways. Everybody loves to hear about the rule breakers. For example, at age sixteen André Watts substituted for an ailing Glenn Gould at a New York Philharmonic concert conducted by Leonard Bernstein. Watts was so sensational that his career was literally made in an instant: the next day, headlines coast-to-coast proclaimed him as "the great new pianist." Coincidentally, Leonard Bernstein had had the same kind of circumstances fall his way a generation

PIANO FIRSTS

The first pianist ever to perform music from memory was Clara Schumann, nineteenth-century piano virtuoso and wife of composer Robert Schumann. Some people regarded this precedent as being bad form; others even felt it "insulted" the composer. While pianists were expected to know the music thoroughly, there was an accepted convention for having the printed note on the stand. Today, playing the piano from memory for a performance is considered standard practice.

● Jan Dussek, a nineteenth-century pianist and composer, gave a concert in Prague in 1804 at which he was the first pianist to sit with his profile to the audience in performance. A handsome man as well as a fine virtuoso, Dussek wanted to show his admiring public his best side. Concert artists today always sit in performance with their right profiles to their audiences.

● While Camille Saint-Saëns was the earliest-born pianist ever to record, Landon Ronald was the *first* pianist to record—he premiered by playing the "Liebestod" from Wagner's *Tristan.*

● Franz Liszt was the inventor of the modern recital and the first musician to give a concert without assistance from other artists. Liszt also began the tradition of using a piano bench for a concert, instead of the usual hard-back chair.

● Jerry Lee Lewis was the first to bring rock 'n' roll piano to millions, which he did in the 1950s. Lewis would get so carried away with his passion for the piano that he would actually attack the instrument during some concerts, a precedent later followed by performers such as The Who and Keith Emerson.

Clara Schumann

Jerry Lee Lewis during his opening night performance at the Cafe de Paris, June 10, 1958

earlier, when he stepped in at a moment's notice for Bruno Walter and conducted the New York Philharmonic.

Not every pianist, however, immediately finds the kind of music that suits his or her expressive style and personality. Like most jazz pianists, Chick Corea came up through the tradition of improvised music. "For me, music has always been more of a way to compose, to get to a new idea, and a tool, which I think should always be." But recently Corea has been leading chamber groups with some of the top classical musicians playing today. The experience has made him want to gain some of the skills from the classical domain and requires of him a totally different musical approach.

Tim Gorman of the Who

LES BONNES TETES MUSICALES

Le petit prodige.

Jan Hammer went to a "hard-core classical musical school," the Academy of Music in Prague, Czechoslovakia, where the composer Dvořák once taught. Although he plays more freely now, "I know that I won't do anything against certain rules that apply to all music—counterpoint, form, harmony, melody, composition—craft."

One pianist who has been able to "cross over" into new domains is the French pianist, Claude Bolling. Obsessed with American jazz from an early age, Claude played in clubs—there was an influx of American jazz at the time—and picked up jazz easily. He recalls: "I fell in love with the music—I never missed a chance to meet any of the great jazz musicians who came to Paris for concerts. When you love something very much, you are always able to do it. That's why I think I adapted so easily to a black American genre."

The story of a teenage boy on the verge of a classical career but encouraged to pursue his own improvisational jazz ideas instead is practically movie material. Peter Nero, who at fifteen was known as Bernie Nierow, was preparing to play Bach and Beethoven for a city-wide musical contest in New York City when one of the judges, critic and pedagogue Abram Chasins, overheard him improvising. After Nero won the competition, whose judges included no less than Vladimir Horowitz, Chasins leveled with him, telling him that his talent for original composition and jazz improvisation were wonderful and rare, something that classical pianists "would give their eyeteeth and lives for."

At the same time Chasins told the boy that his fingers were like "boiled noodles" and badly needed strengthening. Nero embarked on an intense technical program consisting of lessons with Manhattan School of Music piano department head Constance Keene and with Chasins, along with courses in harmony, theory, and orchestration. Three years later Nero could pianistically and technically do almost anything. As a pianist, composer, conductor and arranger, Peter Nero has incorporated his classical background and his feeling for jazz into his arrangement of such popular songs as "Maria," from *West Side Story*, and "Mountain Greenery."

Vladimir Horowitz

Peter Nero

UNUSUAL PIANO PIECES

Irving Berlin, one of America's great songwriters and a natural musician, can only play the piano in one key—the key of F-sharp. Berlin owns a piano that transposes the music for him.

• Composer Claude Debussy carefully dedicated his delightful piano suite, *The Children's Corner*, to his young daughter, Chouchou. The suite comprises six small humorous pieces consecrated to childhood. One of them, "Doctor Gradus ad Parnassum," is a musical picture of Chouchou's piano lesson. It covers the territory unsparingly: the drudgery of the Czerny scales and arpeggios; the student's weary sighs; her discouragement; and then, with playtime coming near, the joyous leap of the two hands ready to bolt and fly.

• Thousands of one-finger piano pieces were written during the nineteenth century and served as parlor entertainment. But the only one of these compositions that remains popular today is "Chopsticks." Published in Glasgow in 1877, this commonplace and sometimes annoying little tune has been borrowed by such outstanding composers as Liszt and Rimsky-Korsakov to show their inventiveness.

• "Carnival of the Animals" by Camille Saint-Saëns is a humorous work representing different animals, as the title implies. But along with selections named for kangaroos, swans, donkeys, chickens, and other livestock, is a short piece called "Pianists." It's a riotous sketch of a musical academy, with mad pianists obviously out of control racing up and down the keyboard practicing their scales and exercises.

• When Charles Ives's *Concord* Sonata and Fourth Symphony are performed, a specially sized block of wood is used by the pianist for striking complex chords directly.

• Twentieth-century composer Henry Cowell wrote piano pieces in which the pianist is supposed to use his elbows, arms, or hands to create unusual harmonic or sound effects.

• In Frederic Chopin's Etude for Piano in G-flat Major, opus 10 no. 5, called, appropriately, the "Black Key Etude," a white key is played only once, in the right hand.

• Chopin's famous "Minute Waltz" (which usually takes a bit more than a minute to perform) was actually written for Georges Sand's dog. Sand was amused by watching her pet dog chasing its tail one day; she begged Chopin, then her "pet" pianist, to set the spectacle to music. He did, and the world is richer for the piece, which is actually subtitled "The Waltz of the Little Dog" ("La Valse du Petit Chien").

Performing

Artur Rubinstein

I cannot tell you how much I love to play for people . . . sometimes when I sit down to practice and there is no one else in the room, I have to stifle my impulse to ring for the elevator man and offer him money to come in and hear me.

Artur Rubinstein (*My Many Years*)

Most pianists develop their own performing personas by preparing idiosyncratically for their moments on stage.

When he concertizes, Lorin Hollander maintains an ascetic way of preparing for "total control and abandon in the musical expression." "I prepare one thousand percent!" he says. He practices in the middle of the night when he's performing. "I'll either have it arranged to get the key to the concert hall, or use a ballroom piano or a mezzanine conference room upright that is at my disposal." He stays at the keyboard and works until his concentration breaks, and then comes back as soon as he regains it. In addition, Lorin states, "two or three hours of sleep before a concert are absolutely necessary. I then wake up, get into the concert clothing [a tuxedo] and go to the hall and work again for an hour or two. Sometimes I do yoga movements or stretching, getting into the larger muscle systems."

On stage Lorin says he never knows what is going to happen. "It is absolutely a mystery whether it's going to be within control, or more or less out of control, but you've done everything possible to be prepared. On the stage it comes down to realizing that this is the moment. You go out there and are totally involved in the moment of the performance: you lay out the overall structure and feel the lines, watching the mind get more or less involved, repairing any damage, having a dialogue with yourself, the higher self, whatever that is."

As the most highly paid performer annually, Liberace says the success of his elaborate show happened gradually. "I began talking to my audiences, which concert pianists didn't do in those days. They were very silent and very serious. I smiled and I talked, and before I knew it I was playing encores that were popular. Eventually humor and other things which made me different crept into my performances. I realized I was developing an individuality most concert pianists don't resort to. They rely on virtuosity and musicianship only. But I have a lot of fun with that. I can reach so many people who normally wouldn't go to a recital." If you can break through the so-called barrier between performer and audience, you're halfway there.

Liberace in full swing

PIANO FEATS

When he was only fourteen, Mozart performed the following musical feats, assisted by just a few professional musicians: He played one of his own symphonies; was soloist for a piano concerto which he sight-read; he sight-read a solo sonata, which he supplied with variations and then transposed into a different key; composed an aria, sang it, and accompanied himself; improvised a sonata from a theme provided for him; improvised a fugue; played the violin in a trio; and conducted one of his own concertos while a soloist at the keyboard.

Mozart at the age of seven years

Art Tatum at the Metropolitan Opera House, January 26, 1944

Jazz pianist Art Tatum had a reputation for incredible pianistic feats which became known after he came to New York in 1932 as accompanist for singer Adelaide Hall. Legend has it that classical piano virtuosi used to frequent New York jazz clubs to hear him. Tatum was predominantly a soloist who used the keyboard as an orchestra to create arrangements such as *Tiger Rag*. Born with cataracts, blind in one eye and with diminishing vision in the other, Tatum was nonetheless a joyous performer whose improvisations were filled with melodic, harmonic, and rhythmic ideas. Pianist Fats Waller was once giving a concert when he spotted Art Tatum in the audience and made a comment that has become Tatum's epithet: "I play the piano, but God is in the house."

The extraordinary pianist Vladimir Horowitz is known for his fiery intensity and the power and drama of his performances. Once, in the 1920s, when he played Rachmaninoff's Third Concerto for the composer, the latter described Horowitz's playing

Ignaz Jan Paderewski

by saying: "He pounced on the concerto with the voraciousness of a tiger and swallowed it whole."

André-Michel Schub feels that while it is thrilling to walk out on stage the artist must keep himself focused, imagining the ideal situation and how he thinks the music should sound. Schub stays aware of what is going on around him. For example, he explains, in Ravinia, where the Chicago Symphony plays in the summer, there's a train that runs right through the middle of the grounds. Invariably, "it will toot at the softest moment—it's inevitable in a slow movement, a real, lyrical spot. It's amazing, while you're playing, you're really not that aware of it. In fact, the choo-choo is part of the charm of playing at Ravinia."

Solo pianists often play with the knowledge that everything rests on their shoulders. As popular composer-pianist Rupert Holmes points out, "There are very few art forms anymore where one person can take all the blame—and all the credit, for example, in the making of a film. But with a pianist there's only the composer—and

SUPERSTAR PIANISTS

The highest-paid classical concert pianist in history was Ignaz Jan Paderewski, who accumulated a fortune estimated at $5 million, $500,000 of which was earned in a single season (1922–1923).

- Liberace earns more than $2 million for each twenty-six-week season, with a peak of $138,000 earned for a single night's performance at Madison Square Garden.
- Considered today's superstar classical pianist, Vladimir Horowitz has played before the largest audience at a single performance (including telecasts).
- The largest live audience ever attracted by a solo performer was 750,000 people, when pianist-singer Elton John played in St. Louis at a free concert in July 1982.

Elton John performing before 750,000 people in St. Louis, July 5, 1982

Horowitz and Zubin Mehta

Liberace

Bobby Short

you. And no one's going to say that Mozart's work just wasn't up to snuff. Whatever I do next is whatever I'm going to hear. What I do is create a whole universe."

"I don't think I've ever given a bad performance on the stage," states Peter Nero. "This is what I know how to do—this is what I'm here for. I've played concerts where I've had zero sleep, been up all night traveling to get there. Somehow everything just comes together. Performing is home for me." Peter and the musicians he plays with may feel weary and not even talk to each other before a performance. But on stage, "we summon up all our energy. What we've been doing subconsciously is storing it up. Because we know that that's why we're going through all of this—to be able to communicate to the audience."

Bobby Short feels that "people are so willing, so capable of being touched. They come to you, and they're so grateful. I find it's a very gratifying endeavor."

Even before an audience starts to applaud, Ruth Laredo can tell what it is like. Ruth gets worried if, before going out on stage, she notices that there's no sound in the hall. "That means people are inhibited. If there's a nice gentle buzz, if they're all talking to each other before the concert, that's normal. It means you've got a chance. When an audience is really with you, it gives you a wonderful energy that helps you to achieve things you might never have achieved before."

All during his life, Artur Rubinstein's communication with an audience was extremely direct, almost palpable. "I felt that special secret current between the public and me, the current which inspires me when I play. There is a moment where I please them all. I can do anything. I can hold them with one little note in the air, and they will not breathe because they wait to hear what happens next in the music. That is a great, great moment. It doesn't always happen, but when it does, it is a great moment in our lives."

Rubinstein has compared the act of performing with lovemaking. "At every concert, I leave a lot to the moment. I want to risk, to dare. It's like making love—the act is always the same, but each time it's different." He always urged musicians, and inspired everyone else, to think and act big. "If you say something, say it with passion and pleasure. Piano playing is a dangerous life. It must be lived dangerously. Take chances, take what comes. The world hates a coward. Who can always play safe? Who wants to? Plunge, give yourself entirely to your art and to your audiences. No one can resist that. And," he concluded, "if you don't lose five pounds and ten drops of blood, you haven't played a concert."

The Mozart family

Mademoiselle Gachet at the Clavier by Vincent van Gogh, 1890

Billy Joel

Billy Joel, who's been nicknamed the "Piano Man," was asked in an interview with *Musician* magazine if he was proud of his piano playing. Joel replied, "Most of the people who play piano in rock 'n' roll aren't pianists, they're piano bangers, and I fit into the latter category." He stated that he plays the piano in a very athletic way, "because I get off on that in concert. I'm too absorbed in the music to be concerned with the musician. I've always sublimated whatever virtuosity I might possibly have in favor of the song."

Lyle Mays, of the Pat Metheny jazz group, likes to hook up with the audience on many levels. "The first thing is, I like to share the joy of music with people. I love to listen to it, and I love to play it." Mays feels that good music should communicate to nonmusicians as well as musicians. "It shouldn't be so complicated that it should be denied. Maybe it's the drama that communicates, or the emotions. We get across to trained musicians also. It's not simple music. But yet it has universality—we try to have that."

"Sometimes the audience goes with you—there's a close bond between you," explains classical pianist Rudolf Firkusny. "It's almost like a religious ceremony, where the priest and the congregation are all together, and I have the feeling that everyone is involved."

Malcolm Frager feels that you have to reach the point where your sense of the audience doesn't affect the performance. "If you're looking for appreciation, you will, unfortunately, respond to a lack of it. Whereas, if you go out onto the stage with the feeling that you've got something you really want to share with the audience—you want to show them what you yourself have discovered about the music—then you're not too concerned about their response to you." Frager adds, "I think it's similar to what you experience in life. If you look for love, you may never find it. But if you go out into life with a feeling of love toward others, you'll have it. The same with musical recognition."

The separation and stiffness between a classical pianist and his audience is something quite a few musicians would like to see eased up. Misha Dichter feels that his generation of pianists—now in their thirties—has come a long way in opening things up. "We don't tour and expect regal treatment or adoration from the public as the older generation sometimes did. Rock stars have it now." Dichter feels that pianists now think of themselves as being part of the audience rather than above it. "But I think the concert should be something special about to happen. I think it's better than coming out and talking about some things, then saying, 'I think I'll play you a Beethoven sonata now.' It gives people a sense that something more profound is going to happen. The lights go down; I think your heart beats a bit faster. Not because I'm going to play a piece, but because you're going to hear a Schubert sonata. I feel that's OK."

Malcolm Frager

OFFBEAT PIANO PERSONALITIES

Classical pianist Glenn Gould's eccentricities were part of his legend. They included the gloves, scarf, and overcoat he wore, even in the summer; the piano stool he took with him everywhere he played, which enabled him to sit low at the keyboard—at eye level; his humming and singing as he played; and his quirky phrasing and unconventional tempos. He was extremely protective of his hands. He once begged off shaking a friend's hands by saying, "Oh, please excuse me. I'm not shaking hands this year."

- The composer and pianist Eric Satie, who used to play in Montmartre piano bars, was known for his peculiar sense of humor and eccentricities. When he died, his friends went to his house and discovered that he had several hundred umbrellas.
- Polish-born Natalia Janotha was an energetic, uninhibited type who became court pianist in Berlin in 1885. Janotha refused to give a concert without her dog, Prince White Heather, somewhere on stage within her view. She would also place a prayer book ostentatiously on the piano.
- Fear of performing—topophobia—is a common ailment among performers. But one virtuoso pianist of the nineteenth century, Adolph von Henselt, carried it to an extreme. He was so terrified of performing that when playing with an orchestra he would hide in the wings until the

opening tutti was over, then rush out and pounce on the piano. On one occasion in Russia he forgot to put out the cigar he was smoking and played the concerto while puffing away, much to the amusement of the Czar. Even the thought of performing made Henselt sick. He gave very few concerts throughout his career—far fewer than any of the other great pianists of the time. Apparently, in the last thirty-three years of his life he gave only three concerts.

- Our modern-day classical piano eccentric has got to be Vladimir Horowitz. For instance, for years Horowitz fans knew that Mr. Horowitz would only give a concert at 4:30 P.M. on a Sunday. However, he recently created a stir by actually giving an evening performance. Tickets are snapped up as soon as a Horowitz performance is announced. People will wait in line for hours to buy tickets, and Horowitz has sometimes appeared at the hall to deliver coffee to his adoring fans. Horowitz has had his piano action speeded up so that it is as light and responsive as possible. Pianists say that in typewriter terms, his piano is an electric as opposed to the manual of most pianists.

- The very talented Elton John often displays extravagant stage antics and costumes. Says Elton, whose real name is Reg Dwight, "As a child, I was fat—about 200 pounds—and I had a terrible inferiority complex. That's why I'm so outrageous on stage, I think, and why I wear ridiculous clothes. I'm catching up for all the games I missed as a child."

Elton John

Performing is a challenge for Jan Hammer. "It's something like trying to make a tornado happen. Once it gets going, you can be swept up in it. It permeates your system—especially if you go out for more than a week. You get into a cycle. If, say, you play for two weeks and have a day off, you get all edgy. At nighttime your hands itch, you want to get out there and do it again, because you've grown into the rhythm of it every day. Performing is habit-forming."

Samuel Sanders performs as accompanist for musician Itzhak Perlman, cellist Yo Yo Ma, and conductor Mstislav Rostropovich, as well as with his own chamber group. Unlike a painter or a writer, says Sanders, a performer can't hide. "Very often I've had a recurring dream," Sanders admits, "and I wonder how many musicians have had the same one. I'm on stage and I discover that I don't have my trousers on! You're terribly vulnerable when you're performing."

Critic Abram Chasins agrees that when an artist walks out on stage, "there's nothing but himself. He's totally naked. The inside of him is what's going to hit the audience. Someone might play phenomenally, and you might say, 'Very interesting,' and never come back to hear him again. Because something deep inside of you was *not* touched, was *not* moved, was *not* excited. The imagination didn't take fire." How do you know when you've been to a truly great performance? According to Chasins, "You get outside, wherever you are, and you look around and say, 'What the hell is this? What are buses? What city am I in? Who are these people?' "

A Manhattan street performance

André Watts

Pianist Jorge Bolet, who also heads the Curtis Institute's piano department, confesses that he is "never, never satisfied with my performances. I'm always delighted when some knowledgeable musical lover comes backstage and says, 'I've heard you so many times. I have never heard you so beautifully as tonight.' That makes me very, very happy." But he says he always stresses in his teaching and with himself that "Our standards are perfection. We musicians are striving for a goal that we know we can never reach. But the day we stop striving for that perfection, that is the day when what I call 'musical rot' sets in—that's the beginning of the end."

André Watts believes that music doesn't communicate when performers are afraid. "The way to get the most out of yourself and out of other people is to be willing for people to throw rotten eggs at you. If you want to keep making music for people, you've got to spend the rest of your life allowing for the possibility that somebody will throw rotten eggs at your soul."

George Gershwin was the only pianist I ever heard who could make a piano laugh. He had a real love affair with music.

Abram Chasins (music critic and pianist)

George Gershwin vacationing in Miami Beach, February 19, 1930

Pianists are very privileged people to have a place where we confront existence: torment, anger, fear, terror, vertigo, and the negative experiences—the devils—in order to bring forth an ecstatic emotional experience. Human existence is both: the transcendent and the fear, like a Bosch painting or a Blake drawing. How dare we think that we can play Bach without confronting the total experience of that?

Lorin Hollander (pianist)

When I play the piano, I'm in another world. It's a kind of trance. The weight of the world is gone. In those forty-five to fifty minutes of playing, I know paradise.

Tania Maria (jazz pianist and singer)

My goal is not just to be a better musician, but to be a better human being. That includes being a superior musician, a superior husband, a superior father, a superior citizen. I don't mean superior to anybody else—it's compared to what I was. That's why human beings have the ability to choose—it's what differentiates us from animals. We're the only beings that are not born into the natural rhythm of the universe. Plants have it. Whatever we do, it adds up within the rhythm of the universe. What I'm saying is, we can contribute more to the positive rhythm; we can add to it, instead of taking away.

Herbie Hancock (jazz pianist and composer)

Gems of American Life.

3

PIANO STUDY

Lightning Strikes, but Who Knows Where or When?

The National Guild of Piano Teachers, the leading American organization of piano teachers, reports that the number of piano students belonging to their association has increased 500 percent over the last fifteen years. Even more astonishing are the results of a survey conducted by the Rockefeller Foundation: Of 30 million pianos in America, about 90 percent are not played. In discussing the implications of this survey, a national magazine commented that piano playing is "the most failed social skill in America." To remedy this situation, a nonprofit educational group called the Piano Consortium was set up to offer piano courses based on playing by ear, rather than on rote memorization. These courses are taught in colleges and universities all over the country. One of the major texts used has an appropriate title: *How to Play the Piano Despite Years of Lessons.* Several piano teachers are in accordance with this method.

"You can play Beethoven for twelve years and not know a thing about the organization of the piano," remarks jazz piano educator John Mehegan. "The first thing to understand is that there are twelve notes in a chromatic scale, each one a focal point of a key, each key with its own coloration and texture. The teacher should

Adele Marcus

make harmony and theory a living, pulsating, fascinating thing, which it is—instead of some dry nonsense or a tome of boredom."

Adele Marcus, a faculty member of the Juilliard School in New York, feels that the teachers themselves need education: "Liszt taught, Chopin taught, Beethoven taught. There's no law that says you're going to lose all of your artistic ability if you teach—on

Manhattan School of Music master class taught by pianist John Browning

the contrary. Teaching takes everything you've got," she says. "You have to summon up all of your creative prowess in order to tap the resources and the potential of the student, and then handle it creatively." She adds: "I walk around with my musical Geiger counter looking for the uranium."

One of the great piano teachers of the century, who trained Aaron Copland, Virgil Thompson, and Elliott Carter, started her students off by having them study harmony. Nadia Boulanger tried to instill a feeling of the long line—a sense of the whole work—and a dynamic rhythm. She believed that students should approach the art of music with serious rigor but, at the same time, with affectionate joy. Her students were guided not only by her precepts and teaching practice but also by her generous nature.

The pioneering methods of Shinichi Suzuki, a noted Japanese violinist and educator, and composer Emile Dalcroze are now being used on young pianists. These methods unlock emotional expression and give the pianist the immediate gratification of making music. They do not introduce a new skill to children; rather, they free a native one by tapping natural rhythmic and melodic abilities. "Ear first, notation later," Suzuki's motto proclaimed; he recognized that just as a child first learns speech by imitating his elders, so too could he learn music.

Constance Keene, head of the piano department at the Manhattan School of Music, often uses a similar visualization process in her teaching: "I base so much of my teaching on having an aural concept, having in mind what you want to present, because otherwise what you play can shock you." The wrong things will come out, she fears, or the right things won't. "You have to always hear it in your mind."

Fritz Jahoda, former chairman of the Music Department at New York's City College, also feels it's immaterial whether you have your wrists high or low or your fingers closed. The main thing is that "you have to listen to yourself."

One of the pioneers in identifying the visualization techniques was Luigi Bonpensiere, and in his book *New Pathways to Piano Technique* he stressed this point: "Never think of your music in terms of execution (of what your hands and fingers should or are going to do) but in terms of interpretative rendering (what you would expect it to sound like if a performer from heaven were executing it for you)."

Lorin Hollander states that, unfortunately, most music lessons are still taught in the traditional manner. "We give a musical instrument to a child so that he will learn the mechanics of it." Lorin feels this is "one of the most treacherous experiences. In those magic moments when somehow the children start to raise emotions and ideas,

and express things they haven't before, if they miss a note, they suddenly get a stage fright. They feel the grownups are being critical. They become afraid and that often closes them in and shuts them down—for good."

Many new pianists are skipping the formative technical phase of piano study by means of electronic keyboards which automatically handle some of the fingerwork for the keyboard player. Composer and pianist Bob James, who teaches music at the esteemed Interlochen Summer Music Camp, feels that it's better to have a solid education on the piano before playing the synthesizer. "It's tempting to bypass all that other rigorous education that's mostly centered around European classical music," he admits. But, on the other hand, "The best education so far is studying the masterpieces in the history of music. That should prepare one theoretically as an overall musician for any stylistic area one wants to choose."

The making of a great concert pianist may depend far more upon his or her environment than upon innate talent, according to a study conducted by Professor Benjamin Bloom of the University of Chicago. He found that the major factors in motivating children were home-instilled values and the encouragement and support a child receives at an early age.

What about the fierce competition that is so frequent among piano students? Pianist Ursula Oppens echoes the views of her professor at Juilliard, Rosina Lhevinne. Madame Lhevinne, as her students called her, was a great teacher, according to Oppens, and one of her great qualities was her attitude toward the world at the time. "She was in her early eighties," says Oppens, "but she was learning all the time and having new ideas. She was interested in talking about new things, new social attitudes, relations between men and women. She was concerned with questions like civil rights. I had always been afraid that being a pianist might have nothing to do with the

EXTREME PRACTICING

Vladimir de Pachmann, a legendary pianist of the late nineteenth and early twentieth centuries, said while in his seventies that it would never do to let his fingers stiffen. He claimed that milking cows was better finger exercise than anything devised by the human mind.

● Another enfant terrible of the nineteenth century, Alexander Dreyschock, would practice sixteen hours a day with his left hand alone and could play octaves as fast, and as smoothly, as single-note passages.

● Robert Schumann was the first well-known pianist who injured his hands out of zeal for the piano. He had to abandon the idea of a performing career, but, to the subsequent joy of music lovers, he dedicated himself instead to being a composer. Several famous contemporary pianists, including Leon Fleisher and Gary Graffman, who were swept away by this kind of piano zeal have spent years recovering their precious hands in an era when science and advanced psychology could come to their rescue.

● The great jazz pianist Art Tatum used to practice away from the keyboard by running filbert nuts across his fingers like a magician.

real world. She had a very good attitude toward competition. She thought competition was good if it made you work harder, and that it didn't matter whether you won or lost."

Music school differs from virtually any other school, with the possible exception of art school, according to pianist-songwriter Rupert Holmes. "If you want to be a doctor, you try to get good grades in biology and chemistry, but no one expects you to be able to perform a minor tracheotomy at age eighteen." But with musicians, says Holmes, "by eighteen you've got to be a semiprofessional. You can't just say, 'I've always had a hankering for piano. I think I'll go to the Manhattan School of Music.' No, you've got to be able to be as good as half the people there already, or at least within striking distance."

Juilliard teacher Adele Marcus has produced scores of competition winners and fine concert pianists, and knows the demands that the musical world will make on her topflight students.

"There's an enormous amount of talent around now, more than ever," says Miss Marcus. "On the other hand, talent is only one part of having a career. There has to be a sense of discipline, the willingness to sacrifice certain things in order to be ready for a career. They expect young people to have in their repertoire everything from Buxtehude to Boulez, if not beyond that. The old guard didn't have that. Mr. Horowitz

Lorin Hollander teaching at Manhattan School of Music

even admitted that in his whole career he only recorded four or five piano concerti. Today you walk into a manager's office and hear, 'If you don't say that you've got fifteen concerti that you can play within a period of two days, forget it.' "

If you are searching for a piano teacher, a companion for duets, or an accompanist, here are ideas that may help you:

Interview teachers, ask for recommendations, or look for advertisements on bulletin boards at local music schools and stores.

Your neighborhood church organist or synagogue cantor may know of or be a good teacher.

At the next concert you attend, ask the pianist, if you liked the person's playing, whether he or she would take you on as a pupil, or whether he or she has any suggestions. If you can't get to the pianist, write a letter or send a demo tape.

Place an ad in local stores or papers. Be specific about the kind of teacher and teaching method you are looking for.

INSPIRING PIANO STUDY THOUGHTS OF THE DAY

One of the very important things is to get the pupil to see results immediately—what we call immediate gratification. That person walks out of a lesson with the feeling of having achieved something or learned something absolutely new—at every lesson. I get the student to feel, "I can do it" and "I *do* do it." My job is to *empower* my students.

Estelle Parnas Oringer (piano teacher and pianist)

Always play as if a master were present.

Robert Schumann (nineteenth-century composer, pianist, and teacher)

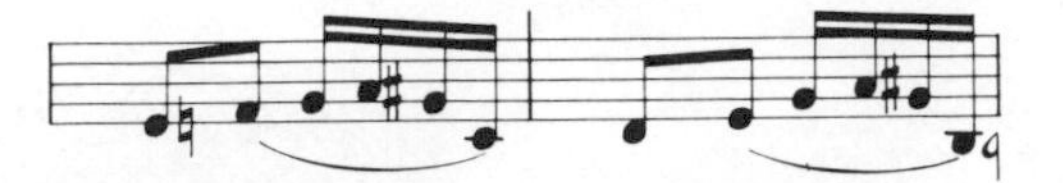

I tell my students it's worth sticking with the piano. There are times when they won't like it—do it anyway! I say to them. I asked my mother if I could give up the piano because everybody else was giving up piano lessons. She just looked at me and said, "Absolutely not." I will thank her to my dying day for forcing me to continue.

Sheila Mayer (piano teacher and pianist)

I don't look for winners, particularly. I look for people who really relate to music, where it means that they couldn't *live* without it. That's my barometer.

Adele Marcus (Juilliard piano teacher)

Two Young Girls at the Piano
by Auguste Renoir

The Piano Workout: Does Practice Make You Perfect?

Not every pianist will feel comfortable with Thomas Edison's often repeated formula for genius: "One percent inspiration, ninety-nine percent perspiration." Yet, to acquire a solid technique, you do need to put in your ninety-nine percent.

"When I'm at home, I have a rigid schedule," says rock pianist Tim Gorman. "I practice six hours a day: two hours are spent with technique, two on sight-reading, and two are for composing—either on a synthesizer or an acoustic piano. I try to sight-read as much as possible to keep my chops [technique, in rock talk] in shape. It doesn't matter if you make mistakes. The important thing is to keep going." He sight-reads the three B's (Bach, Beethoven, and Brahms) and performs plenty of Hanon and Czerny exercises. Tim tries to breathe with the instrument and to produce a good tone from the string, "actually trying to feel as if it were singing or being bowed, rather than being hammered. A lot of it for me is ideo-kinetics. I get an idea in my mind and I really try to see it through that day, and if it seems to start working, I'll keep doing it every day."

To work on her technique, rock 'n' roller Bonnie Hayes of Bonnie Hayes & the Wild Combo plays Pischna exercises and Bach fugues "with a great deal of attention to detail." She takes jazz solos from records, transposes the chord progressions into every key, and improvises. "When I work out, I try to do five or six hours a day. It becomes very enjoyable."

Classically trained Peter Schott has this advice for aspiring pianists-keyboardists: "Practice a lot by yourself, even before you play with others. And learn everything, not just one area of music."

The elegant jazz pianist Teddy Wilson, who played with Benny Goodman and Sarah Vaughan, spoke about how he keeps those amazing fingers in shape. "I practice exercises, bits of Chopin études, Moszkowski études, and Bach inventions. I also use a relaxation exercise that was taught to me years ago by a student of Tobias Matthay, as well as exercises by Carl Tausig, who was a student of Liszt."

Misha Dichter says he's done a lot of thinking about whether or not there's a correct hand position. "The traditional position I was taught was that having rounded fingers was correct—you weren't supposed to break your joints. The old-fashioned system they used to use was to push a sharp pencil into the palm of the student to achieve an arch." But, he says, "I've almost gone flat in my hand position." Influenced by Horowitz, he adds, "It makes an incredible amount of sense—there is no loss of motion, the fingers are always in flat contact with the key, which means there's a greater percentage of finger on the key at all times, so the chance for error is greatly reduced. I already thought I had reached my technical limit. But suddenly, with this

new approach to the hand position and other insights, I feel that a wall has fallen away. I can't even listen to things I did three years ago—I can play so much better now!"

How does jazz pianist Joanne Brackeen keep in shape, making sure her fingers are limber? "I just do it," she says simply. "How do you keep your legs in shape so you can walk? I guess if you don't walk for a long time, it's hard to walk. I'm busy playing. Sometimes I don't have any time to work out on the piano, but I always like to spend as much time as possible there." Her playing sounds thunderous—how does she achieve that? "Yeah, that's me, whether I'm at the piano or not. That's the way I feel about being alive. So it's not in the fingers, it's in the being of the person, the fingers are only a little part of you." A very impassioned way of looking at things. "Yes, that's what this business of being on the planet is."

Artur Rubinstein expressed regret about having been lazy in his younger days. "I was unwilling to practice eight, nine, or ten hours a day because I lived for every second." But he questioned the wisdom of young pianists who shut themselves off in practice rooms, oblivious to the world. "You can imagine how a young guy in his twenties feels sitting at a piano for eight hours a day," he said. "To hell with it—if I were he, I would rather become, I don't know what, a dishwasher."

"Practice for a reason, get something out of it," André Watts urges, although he finds it difficult to derive a lot of pleasure from intensive practicing. "I've often said that if I were disposed to signing over my soul to Mephistopheles, as in the Faust legend, and he would give me anything, probably what I would want is the ability to play the notes of any and every piece, so that the only work I would have to do would be the fine work, the music-making work."

AMAZING HANDS

Virtuoso pianist Dinu Lipatti's pinkie was his longest finger, a rare phenomenon indeed.

- World-famous artist Artur Rubinstein was a "born pianist" in every respect, including his hands. He had wide palms and spatulate (or spoon-shape) fingertips; his little finger was almost as long as his middle one; and his hands could reach an extraordinary twelve-note span on the keyboard.
- Sergei Rachmaninoff, the Russian pianist and composer, is considered to have had one of the greatest keyboard spans: twelve whole notes. He could play a left-hand chord of C, E-flat, G, C, and G.
- When pianist Paul Wittgenstein lost his right arm in World War I, composer Maurice Ravel wrote Concerto for the Left Hand so that Wittgenstein could keep playing. Wittgenstein held his audiences spellbound with this classic work, and went on to inspire other one-armed pianists to keep performing. Ravel's Concerto is also used by two-armed pianists to prove their left-hand virtuosity.

SIX MORCEAUX
COMPOSED EXPRESSLY FOR THE
CABINET ORGAN
Nº1 ANTICIPATION
Nº2 REMINISCENCE.
Nº3 PENITENCE.
MASON & HAMLIN CABINET ORGAN
BY
L. H. SOUTHARD.
Nº4 IN MEMORIAM
Nº5 CHILDREN'S MARCH.
Nº6 GAIETY.
Boston Published by OLIVER DITSON & CO. 277 Washington Street

Watts defines good technique as having control and "playing as quietly as you want, slowing down, getting faster, making different sounds within one melody, changing the color. The height of technique probably is being able to make colors."

For classical artist Lorin Hollander, practicing at the piano is a deeply meditative psychological search. "The music is going on below the level of the mind. You have to understand the relationship of the mind to the muscles and to the experience of playing the piano. It is not just the fingers, of course, it is the sense of pulse and rhythm. It is the whole body dancing."

Jorge Bolet compares his highly thought-out and concrete method of learning a new piece of music to photography, a favorite pastime of his. "At first you look at the composition in an overall fashion, with a wide-angle lens: you have to learn the notes and the score, and be able to play the composition at a correct tempo. The more closely you look at the music, the more you use a medium-range telephoto. Before you know it, you're analyzing certain sections of the music with a 500-millimeter reflex lens, then before long, you're looking at a melodic line or harmonic transition with a macro-lens." Finally, he says, "You get to the point where you actually analyze all

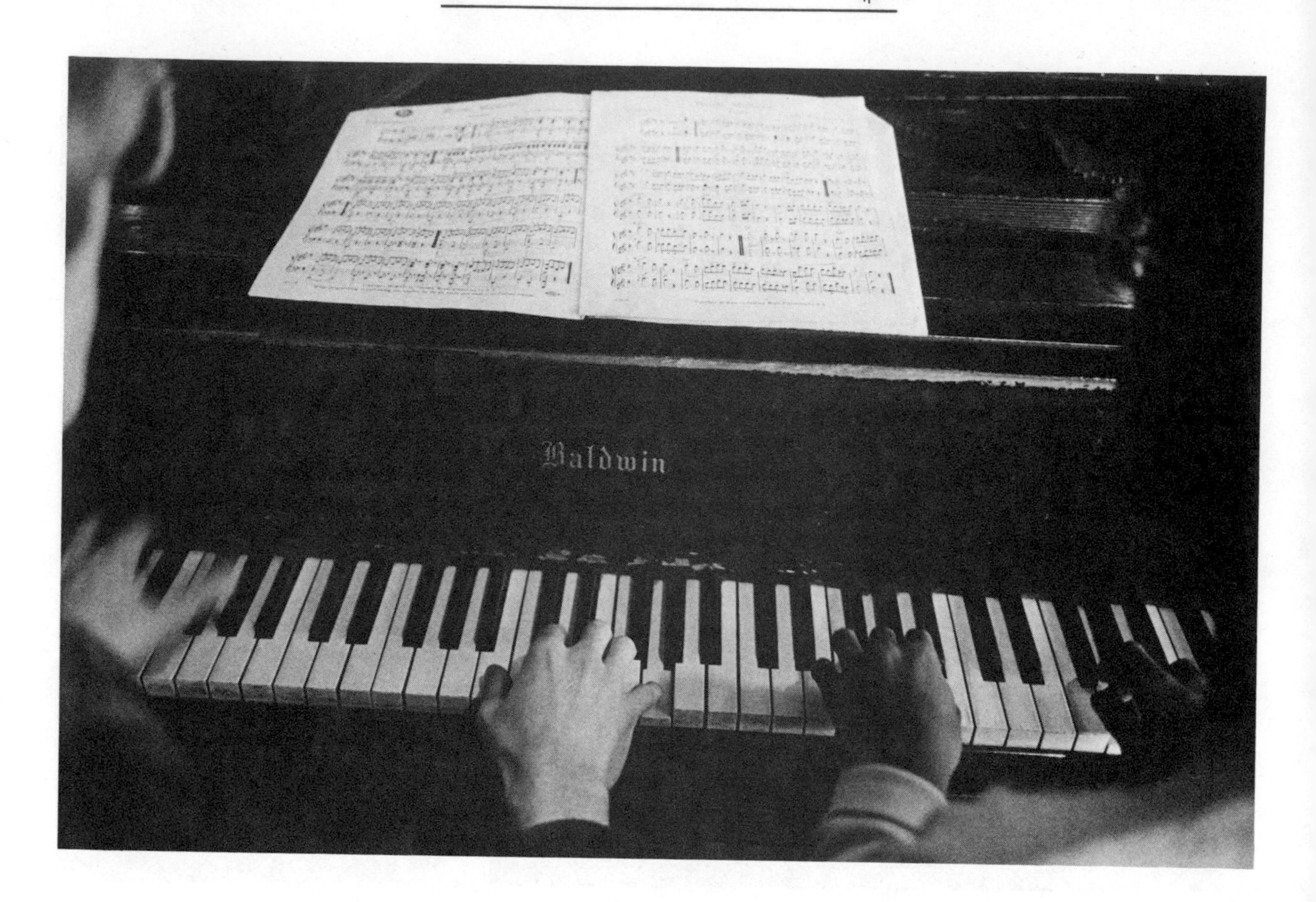

these things under a microscope. Then, of course, it's putting the whole piece of music with all its elements together—and it's the sort of thing you can do over a period of fifty, sixty, seventy years. There's no end to it. It can never *have* an end to it!"

Too much practice, or mis-practice, sometimes has disastrous consequences. Young pianist and potential performer Bennett Morrison suffered a hand injury from overpracticing. Practicing eleven to fourteen hours a day during his turbulent teenage years, he commented, "Other kids turned to drugs and sex. I chose the piano. I was trying so hard to possess it completely, practicing all day long and never stopping, even when my hands were fatigued." None of the doctors could find any particular muscular problems, and none were revealed by neurological tests. But a wise musician friend gave Bennett good advice: He told him not to touch the piano for six months, that his hands were obviously tired and needed a rest. When Morrison finally returned to the piano, eighteen months later, his hands were as good as new.

The discipline needed to practice is often hidden to nonmusicians. A conversation between two men overheard by a concert manager after a British pianist's recital epitomizes this gap. First Man: "The chap plays pretty well, doesn't he?" Second Man: "Well, he ought to. I don't suppose he ever did a day's work in his life!"

THE ART OF LISTENING

Composer Aaron Copland explains that we listen to music on three separate planes: the sensuous plane, where the sheer sound appeal of the music is a "potent and primitive force," the expressive plane, which evokes feelings, and the musical plane, which involves hearing the melodies, rhythms, harmonies, tone colors, and the principles of musical forms. Developing the ability to hear on this musical plane, to actively listen, will most benefit the listener.

Active listening is one of the arts of playing the piano and can make all the difference between competence and brilliance. André Watts believes that one of the distinguishing factors between a pianist and a musician is that the latter listens to himself. He asserts that one's "fast computer, the control computer, the listening computer, keeps running and telling me what it sounds like." As one pianist was playing a piece, her teacher stopped her and said, "You got to the fortissimo (ultraloud) already after only a few bars? Why, there's nothing left for you to do but to kill yourself!"

Like Watts, Copland feels that the ideal listener is both "inside and outside the music at the same moment . . . almost like the composer: carried away by it and yet coldly critical of it."

Creative listening can open one's mind to possibilities that haven't been explored. Lorin Hollander takes listening one step further. "In music," he explains, "if one allows oneself to listen totally to the harmonies, to listen so totally that there are no thoughts in the mind, one can actually feel the body sensations as one hears these harmonies." More surprising yet, he says, "In other words, if you listen to D-flat major and really *listen* to D-flat major, you can feel the body sensations, the muscles almost forming themselves in the shape of D-flat major. One *becomes* D-flat major."

Van Cliburn (right) with Placido Domingo

The Competitions

When Van Cliburn won the Tchaikovsky Piano Competition in Moscow in 1958, his victory was every American pianist's victory. American artists who had previously figured only in national competitions were suddenly acknowledged in the international arena. A career as a pianist was finally considered valid and important. "You were no longer a sissy to take piano lessons if you were a boy," says Jack Romann, head of Baldwin's Concert and Artists Department. "Because here was this six-foot-six-inch-tall, lanky, red-blooded American boy, playing the piano with impunity."

The Van Cliburn story prompted the creation of what is now the most important piano contest in America: the Van Cliburn Competition.

A second major contribution to piano competition occurred in America in 1981, when twenty-eight-year-old pianist André-Michel Schub won the Van Cliburn. Its finale was telecast live by PBS after daily newspapers had kept millions posted of the outcomes of the successive rounds.

The Van Cliburn Competition is more unusual than other competitions in the demands it makes on the pianist's repertoire. The Chopin Competition, for example, requires only Chopin; the Beethoven Competition, in Vienna, is devoted entirely to Beethoven; and the Tchaikovsky, in Moscow, has a strong emphasis on Russian music and on Tchaikovsky's in particular. But the Van Cliburn demands enormous musical and pianistic versatility—from Bach to Bernstein.

Every competitor has the opportunity to play twice, for twenty minutes each time, before anyone is eliminated. Total repertoire requirements add up to about five hours of playing—the equivalent of three or four full recitals! The pianist is not forced to learn specific pieces, and in the first phase of the competition can choose a Bach suite, a Mozart sonata, a Beethoven sonata, a major romantic work, and an impressionistic or contemporary work. In the semifinals, in which twelve pianists are chosen from forty, a new set of pieces is required which includes a one-hour solo recital featuring the mandatory piece, "Touches," which Leonard Bernstein wrote for the event. Only six pianists are selected for the finals, and they must each perform one classical concerto and one romantic concerto one right after the other. Jeffrey Kahane, a Van Cliburn finalist who placed fourth, chose the Mozart E-flat Concerto and the Brahms First Piano Concerto. He commented on the fact that the two concerti would be played a day apart in most competitions. After solo piano performances, chamber music, and concerto with orchestra, the winner is chosen.

A team of twelve international judges consisting of educators, pianists, and musicians rates the pianists on a scale of from 1 to 100 on various pieces, and computers add up the points. Music commentator and author Abram Chasins, a Van Cliburn judge, says he waits for "contestants who make me put my pen down." He listens for a pianist with "style, color, interpretation, ideas, imagination—someone who reveals something new to you." Seymour Lipkin, another Van Cliburn judge, reminds us that "competition judges are awestruck by an individual voice."

Jeffrey Kahane, winner of the 1983 Artur Rubinstein Competition

André-Michel Schub recalls that the Van Cliburn was "as nerve-racking and horrendous an ordeal as anything you can go through. I can't even describe the pressure. After all, I knew the outcome would directly change my career." He considers himself lucky. He has entered only two competitions in his life and won them both: the Naumberg, in 1974, got him launched with concerts and a manager.

At the most recent Van Cliburn Competition in May 1981, pianists came from the United States, Canada, Europe, Asia, South Africa, Israel, Australia, South America, Rumania, Hungary, and China to participate. It lasted two weeks, during which contestants stayed with host families who had vied for the privilege of housing these young musical giants.

Many musicians have become critical of competitions, and feel it is inappropriate to judge musicians like athletes. In a competitive situation, one can't "win" at a Beethoven sonata the way one can at a baseball game or a tennis match. Competitions, they feel, put the spotlight on a handful of talented pianists for the duration of the event, but do nothing for the long-term career-building process for any but the very top-ranked pianists. Not even winning such a prestigious contest as the Van Cliburn can guarantee a career. "For a pianist, there's no job tenure—no job security," Schub states. "Winning has, of course, given me opportunities—more even than I dreamed of." (He's booked solid for the next three years.) "But once you have the concerts, you have to have something to say in them. There has to be a certain individuality in your playing. Being a musician is a lifelong growth process; a competition is just credentials. What you strive for is to make music, to have greater and greater insights and projection of the music."

André-Michel Schub (with cowgirls) celebrates winning the Van Cliburn Competition in Texas

TIMING IS ALL

The longest piano-playing marathon lasted for 1172 hours, twenty-seven minutes (forty-eight days, twenty hours, and twenty-seven minutes), with the pianist playing twenty-two hours every day (with five-minute intervals each playing hour) from January 6 to February 24, 1978. The marathoner was Roger Lavern, who performed at the Osborne Tavern, London.

- The women's record is 133 hours nonstop (five days, thirteen hours) by Mrs. Marie Ashton, in a theater in Northumberland, England, from August 18 to 23, 1958. Her last piece was "Five Minutes More."
- The record time for pitch raising (one semi-tone) and then returning a piano to a musically acceptable quality is four minutes and twenty seconds, accomplished by Steve Fairchild at the Piano Technicians Guild contest at the Dante Piano Company factory, New York, February 5, 1980.
- The longest piano composition is a continuous nonrepetitious piece called "The Well-Tuned Piano," by La Monte Young. It was first presented by the Dia Art Foundation in New York City in 1980. The piece lasted four hours, twelve minutes, and ten seconds.

Virgil Thompson by Marisol

Jorge Bolet

Critics feel that the tremendous pressure of competitions forces the pianists to conform in their playing during and long after an event. Jorge Bolet, head of the Curtis Institute's piano department, finds that competition pianists are all mechanical perfectionists: "They never miss a note, never take a chance, and never have ideas of their own. Go to one of the big international competitions—everybody plays alike." He thinks competitions are responsible for urging pianists to play it safe so as not to antagonize any of the judges. "I say a typical competition winner is one who plays everything very well, which is about the worst thing I can say about any pianist. When you play something and it takes a person's breath away, that's art. The rest is piano playing. Every conservatory is putting piano players out by the dozen. They can play the *Mephisto Waltz* by Liszt, *Islamey* by Balakirev—supervirtuoso pieces—and play them faster than anyone ever thought possible. But what's that?"

Arthur Greene was actually told by a judge at the Busoni Competition to "play the way other people play now." But Van Cliburn founder Irl Allison denied that "competitions breed competition players," and said, "Competitions are developing a feeling for music like nothing else in the world is doing. We certainly need every possible way to keep the classics alive."

Whatever the dissenting viewpoints, many pianists do launch their careers during competitions. "The publicity machine and the press jump at the opportunity to make something of the competition," remarks Jeffrey Kahane, who won the Artur Rubinstein Competition in 1983. He acknowledges that this opens avenues for performances and recordings that young pianists could never have found on their own. A competition circuit has even developed in recent years in which pianists who play at Leeds in England may meet up with each other again at the Busoni in Italy, the Queen Elisabeth in Belgium, or at the Rubinstein in Tel Aviv.

Funny things often happen during competitions, despite the pervasive pressures. "An Italian man who couldn't speak much English came backstage after I had played in the third round of the Busoni," Greene said. "He told me I better do well because he had some money on me! It made me feel great—someone thought I was actually going to win." 'Making book' on competitions is no longer rare. At the Queen

Arthur Greene, Xerox Affiliate Artist Pianist

The Competitions

Competition	When held	Age limits	First prize	Address
Gina Bachauer International Competition	Every 2 years Next one: 1984	18–32	Steinway Grand Piano-Model "L" plus associated performing dates	c/o Brigham Young University C-550 Harris Fine Arts Center Provo, Utah 84602
Busoni International Piano Competition	Annually	15–32	5,000,000 lire	Concourse International de Piano "F. Busoni" Conservatorio "C. Monteverdi" Piazza Domenicani 19 1-39100 Bolzano, Italy
Chopin International Piano Competition	Every 5 years Next one: 1985	17–30	40,000 zlotys	Chopin Competition Committee Krakowskie Przedmieście 15/17 Warsaw, Poland
Van Cliburn International Piano Competition	Every 4 years Next one: 1985	18–30	$12,000 plus Carnegie Hall recital, etc.	Van Cliburn Foundation 3505 W. Lancaster Ft. Worth, Texas 76107
Leeds International Piano Competition	Every 3 years Next one: 1984	Not over 32	Steinway Grand Piano; 2500 pounds	University of Leeds Education Department Leeds, Yorkshire LS1 3 AE, England
Queen Elisabeth of Belgium International Music Competition	Every 2 years Next one: 1985	17–31	250,000 Belgian francs	Count J. P. de Launoit Executive Committee Rue Baron Horta, 11 B-1000 Brussels, Belgium
Artur Rubinstein International Piano Master Competition	Every 3 years Next one: 1986	18–32	$5000, concerts and recording engagements	PO Box 29404 Shalom Tower, 5th Floor Tel Aviv, Israel
Tchaikovsky International Competition	Every 4 years Next one: 1986	16–30	2500 rubles	Organizing Committee 15 Neglinnaya Street Moscow, U.S.S.R.
University of Maryland International Piano Festival & Competition	Annually	16–32	$5000	University of Maryland Office of Summer Programs College Park, MD 20742

Elisabeth Competition in Brussels, where every round is televised, betting is apparently a regular practice. At the Chopin, everyone keeps a scorecard in front of him.

Some competitions represent a successful partnership between the arts and business communities. At the Pepsico-American Jewish Congress Competition in New York City, a small competition with only thirteen contestants and three judges, the winning pianist captured the opportunity to play at the strategic 92nd Street YMHA Auditorium. I attended this competition and watched each pianist play with every fiber of his body, putting all of himself into every note and every phrase, while the judges whispered and made notes. In the middle of a highly expressive theme, a judge would cut in and say, "Can we have the Chopin, please?" The competitor would haul up short, and then, without catching his breath, would launch into a piece that had a completely different mood, feeling and interpretation. Suddenly, after what must have seemed like hours to them, it was all over. He had either won or he hadn't.

Toscanini gives a lesson to his granddaughter, the daughter of Vladimir Horowitz

Leon Greene, Xerox Affiliate Artist Pianist

One competition, which is in fact an audition, could point the way to the future: the Affiliate Artists program, sponsored by the Xerox Corporation. Six pianists are chosen, becoming "Xerox Pianists," and then given jobs, not prizes. They get two-week residencies with major and regional orchestras, and play in small community programs as well. As director Jesse Rosen puts it: "There are hundreds of new performing artists every year. The system of nurturing talent, bringing it out into the world, is horribly deficient in dealing with the quantity of people coming into the profession. We need to provide opportunities for talented pianists to prove themselves."

Artur Rubinstein summed up the irony of the whole competition phenomenon after he had served on the jury of a piano competition. He was asked to rate each pianist between zero and twenty. He did so, giving them either a zero or a twenty. When the chairman of the jury queried him on this, Rubinstein simply shrugged and said, "Well, either they can play the piano or they can't!"

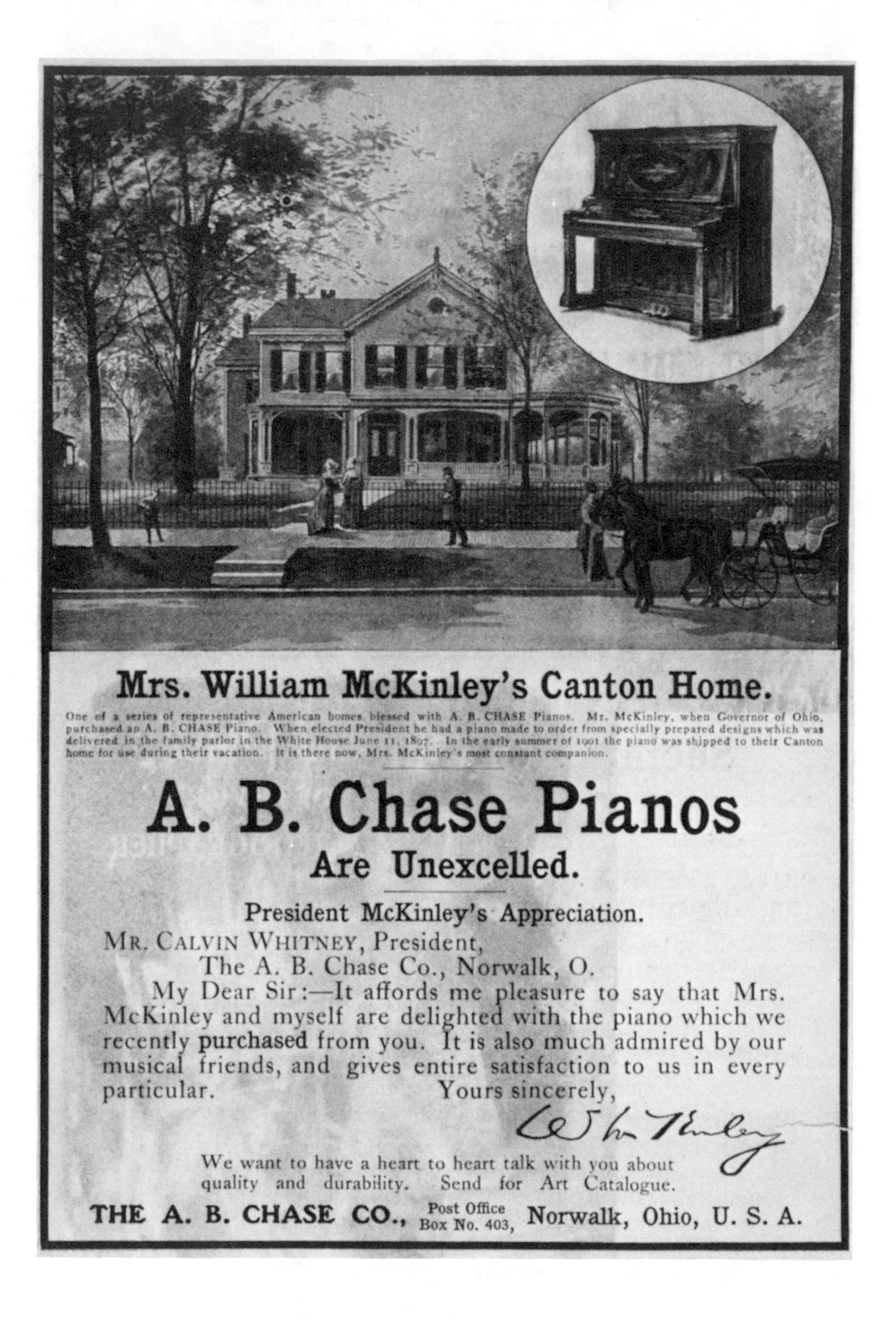
Mrs. William McKinley's Canton Home.
One of a series of representative American homes blessed with A. B. CHASE Pianos. Mr. McKinley, when Governor of Ohio, purchased an A. B. CHASE Piano. When elected President he had a piano made to order from specially prepared designs which was delivered in the family parlor in the White House June 11, 1897. In the early summer of 1901 the piano was shipped to their Canton home for use during their vacation. It is there now, Mrs. McKinley's most constant companion.
A. B. Chase Pianos
Are Unexcelled.
President McKinley's Appreciation.
MR. CALVIN WHITNEY, President,
The A. B. Chase Co., Norwalk, O.
My Dear Sir:—It affords me pleasure to say that Mrs. McKinley and myself are delighted with the piano which we recently purchased from you. It is also much admired by our musical friends, and gives entire satisfaction to us in every particular.
Yours sincerely,
W McKinley
We want to have a heart to heart talk with you about quality and durability. Send for Art Catalogue.
THE A. B. CHASE CO., Post Office Box No. 403, Norwalk, Ohio, U. S. A.

THE PIANO IN OTHER SPHERES

The Piano in Literature

"Don't misunderstand me, please, Miss Landon. I respect beauty in all forms. I appreciate everything in this room, but most of all, I love that big, fat, black lady by the window." He pointed to the grand piano. "To me, she's more interesting than paintings, more subtle than furnishings, more alluring than women with much better legs."

from *Always Is Not Forever,*
by Helen Van Slyke (1977)

Pianos and pianists have come a long way from nineteenth-century literature, in which hopeful females hovered over keyboards, anxious to dazzle their suitors by displaying their musically refined natures. In European and American novels, every proper living room or salon had a piano, which represented the education and romantic and economic ambitions of the upper middle class. In Louisa May Alcott's *Little Women*, Beth, the youngest sister, "could get much music out of the old piano; she had a way of softly touching the yellow keys and making a pleasant accompaniment to the simple songs they sang."

In Jane Austen's nineteenth-century best-seller, *Pride and Prejudice*, "Elizabeth and Mrs. Hurst played the pianoforte while Mr. Darcy looked on and eventually invited her to dance." A girl's matrimonial prospects brightened considerably if she was a pianist. It showed a woman's charm and grace, as well as her romantic, sensual nature. Piano skills did not compensate, however, for a girl's plainness, as Elizabeth's more accomplished friend Mary sadly discovered. Furthermore, it was fine for Elizabeth to play pleasant Scotch and Irish airs, but she did well to stay away from the

Bohemian Lady Playing the Virginal by Wenceslans Hollar (1607—1677)

more forceful piano concertos. The underlying message was clear: Women should not compromise their femininity by playing the piano too well, nor by displaying any other cleverness. In his enlightening book *Men, Women and Pianos*, Arthur Loesser explains that "the history of the pianoforte and the history of the social status of women can be interpreted in terms of one another."

Although women pianists far outnumbered their male counterparts in nineteenth-century novels and in real life, it eventually became safe for men to be portrayed in literature as pianists. They were usually depicted as distinguished and passionate pianists and dazzling virtuosos, like the Liszts and Rubinsteins of the time.

Beethoven's impact on literature was stunning. With his powerful personality, tormented soul, and fraternal spirit, he inspired a half dozen novels. One of the most famous of these is *Jean-Christophe*, a series of novels by Romain Rolland, which shows the main character's development from an unwilling young boy to a composer of major international stature.

> *They sat him down again in front of the piano; and he played, unaccompanied, "The Pleasures of Youth." There was pandemonium afterwards. After every piece, the audience shouted out with enthusiasm; they wanted him to start all over; and he was proud of his success and almost hurt at the same time that the approval seemed like a command. At the end, the whole room got up to acclaim him—the Grand-Duke motioned for applause.*

Marcel Proust's *Remembrance of Things Past* features Professor Vinteuil, who was metamorphosed in the course of the novel-cycle from an insignificant piano teacher to a recognized master of composition. Proust set many of his social scenes in piano salons, as he did here in *Swann's Way,* where the musicians managed to transcend the snobbism and social practices of the period, allowing the frenetically status-conscious salon-goers to reveal their wild and passionate selves:

> *Filled with ironical melancholy, Swann watched them as they listened to the pianoforte intermezzo (Liszt's "Saint Francis Preaching to the Birds"); Mme. de Cambremer, [whom he saw] as a woman who had received a sound musical education, [was] beating time with her head—transformed for a nonce into the pendulum of a metronome, the sweep and rapidity of whose movements from one shoulder to the other (performed with that look of wild abandonment in her eye which a sufferer shows who is no longer able to analyze his pain, nor anxious to master it, and says merely "I can't help it") so increased that at every moment her diamond earrings caught in the trimming of her bodice, and she was obliged to put straight the bunch of black grapes which she had in her hair, though without any interruption of her constantly accelerated motion.*

Two generations later, American writers would bring out the subtlety, romantic allure, and sexual innuendoes of the piano.

Herman Wouk's novel *Marjorie Morningstar* featured a young Marjorie falling in love with piano-playing Noel Airman, the summer camp counselor whom she considered a musical genius:

> *Noel sauntered to the piano. "Wally, stop abusing that instrument and let me at it." The boy slid off the stool without a word and shambled to the table, hands in pockets. . . . Airman began to play the most popular song of the time, a jigging ballad about a brokenhearted lover. He seemed to render it with all seriousness, yet soon everybody around the table was laughing. He emphasized the wrongly placed vowels, the cheap words, the grammatical errors, with faint elegance, and the contrast was killingly funny. Marjorie laughed louder than anyone. She was transported with pleasure at her own acuteness in understanding Airman. She felt she had come into the circle of wit and charm in the world that she had always dreamed of. Airman was a fantastic being in her eyes. . . . She perfectly understood why women were insane about him.*

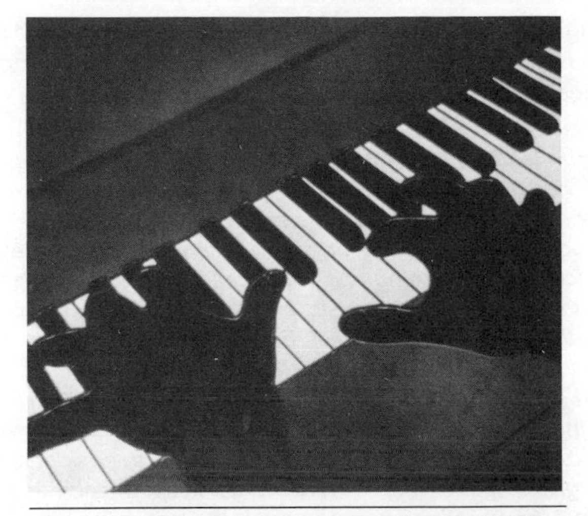

"Improvisation" by Willie Turey

The life of pianist-composer Edward MacDowell is the subject of *Chamber Music*, a contemporary novel by Doris Grumbach. The pianist is portrayed as a tortured artist and misunderstood musician.

In Thomas Thompson's gory novel *Blood and Money*, one of the characters, a plastic surgeon, also happens to be a pianist, an avid music lover, and the proud owner of an expensive Bösendorfer piano and a $100,000 private music room. But he's got a Jekyll-and-Hyde personality: by day the doctor-pianist seduces his female clients and mistresses with his sweet, romantic piano music. By night he slowly poisons his wife, Joan, with the most odious medical methods imaginable, eventually killing her.

> *The average patient who visited John's office would probably not even notice the art, so dazzling was the young doctor's personal style. Particularly if the patient was an impressionable older woman. She would be invited to sit on the sofa while John Hill poured her a glass of wine. There would be small talk of music and perhaps of Joan's latest accomplishments in the horse shows. Then John would move to the piano he had installed near his desk and he would play, perhaps, a soothing Chopin sonata. Finally the conversation would move to the annoying bags that had come so rudely to the woman's eyes. With a thumb so light it seemed made of cobwebs and dusting powder, he would touch the blemishes and murmur his confidence that a quick and easy operation would banish the bags and the wrinkles. . . . He operated with style. While music in an operating theatre is not unusual . . . John Hill rigged up a stereo system that he could carry from hospital to hospital. Installing it in a corner . . . John inserted classical music cassettes. One patient spoke of the experience. "The last thing I remember was that gorgeous doctor bending over me, and Beethoven crashing all around me."*

Paula Gosling's murder mystery *Solo Blues*, published in 1981, concerns a jazz pianist fighting to make his comeback as a classical pianist as he moves in and out of contrasting musical worlds.

> *After a few moments, Johnny lifted his hands and began the bouncing, syncopated rhythm of the opening. He heard some gasps rise like a flight of startled moths from the audience. He was right, they knew their music. And then he didn't hear anything else except the shade of old Maurice Ravel breathing over his shoulder. The bastard had always had it in for concert pianists, and the "Alborada" was one of his most fiendish legacies to the breed he called "circus performers." He and Maurice kept waiting for him to blow it and they were both disappointed. Short of actually falling off the bench, there didn't seem to be anything he could do wrong. His hands felt weightless, electric, alive. He watched them almost disinterestedly as they skittered over the keys, grabbing the notes in chunks, yet keeping each one separate and distinct. Eventually they cut through the last rising phrase with razor precision and dropped into his lap. He stared at them and then at Gessler as the audience went berserk. Jesus Christ, Laynie was right. He* could *still do it.*

Poets have also been inspired by the piano. D. H. Lawrence wrote romantically about his piano memories.

Softly, in the dusk, a woman is singing to me;
Taking me back down the vista of years, till I see
A child sitting under the piano, in the boom of the tingling strings
And pressing the small, poised feet of a mother who smiles as she sings.

from "Piano," *Collected Poems* (1929)

The modern poet Wallace Stevens found a perfect harmony between music and love.

Just as my fingers on these keys
Make music, so the selfsame sounds
On my spirit make a music, too.

Music is feeling, then, not sound;
And thus it is that what I feel,
Here in this room, desiring you,

Thinking of your blue-shadowed silk,
Is music.

from "Peter Quince at the Clavier" (1967)

Other literary works in which pianos play major and minor roles:
The Kreutzer Sonata; *Anna Karenina* by Leo Tolstoy
A Doll's House by Henrik Ibsen
Against the Grain (A Rebours) by J. K. Huysmans
The Great Gatsby by F. Scott Fitzgerald
Dr. Faustus by Thomas Mann
Point Counterpoint by Aldous Huxley
Thanking My Mother for Piano Lessons by Diane Wakoski
Cassandra at the Wedding by Dorothy Baker
Solo by Jack Higgins
The Piano by Aníbal Monteiro Machado
The Painted Lady by Françoise Sagan

THE PIANO IN FILM

Filmmakers from Hollywood to Stockholm have cast the piano in illustrious roles. It has been featured in Busby Berkeley musical extravaganzas, used as a symbolic presence in artistic films, and has provided an intangible backdrop to countless love stories and murder mysteries. It sets the tone for a myriad of feelings, eras, events, characters, and motifs in motion pictures.

Harpo Marx in *A Night at the Opera*

Sam playing it again in *Casablanca*

Ingrid Bergman, as a young pianist, and Leslie Howard, as an older violinist, in *Intermezzo*

Hoagie Carmichael and piano in *To Have and Have Not*

Dancing to the songs of George Gershwin in *The King of Jazz*

Frederick Chopin

Franz Liszt

Politics and the Piano

Since antiquity, emperors and kings have summoned their greatest musicians and entertainers to perform in their courts. Music offers world leaders—and everyone else—a moment of bliss, beauty, happiness, and even enlightenment. Music is a part of every festive or tragic occasion, whether it be the Welsh anthem written for the marriage of Prince Charles and Lady Diana or Samuel Barber's "Adagio for Strings," played at the funeral of Princess Grace of Monaco, underscoring universal grief.

There are those world leaders who not only listen to music but are musicians themselves. As a boy, Harry Truman arose at five o'clock in the morning to practice the piano. He studied with a Kansas City pianist whose teacher, Theodor Leschetizky, had, in turn, trained another politician, Ignaz Jan Paderewski, who was not only a premier of Poland but also one of the nineteenth century's greatest virtuosos. Paderewski once used one of his own compositions, a minuet, to give Truman a piano lesson. Years later Truman performed the minuet at Potsdam, the site of the peace talks which helped conclude the Second World War. Truman's audience members were no less than Churchill and Stalin. Stalin appreciated the performance, Truman said later, but Churchill, not so much—"that kind of music" apparently didn't interest him.

Other keyboard-playing presidents have included Richard Nixon, who played "just for fun" and invited greats such as Duke Ellington to the White House to play along with him. Thomas Jefferson, who was a violinist, may have brought over one of the very first pianos in American history: he had originally ordered a clavichord as a gift for a woman he was courting, but, sensing the piano's promise, changed the request.

Current pianist-politicians find it hard, though, to practice both arts simultaneously. Former congresswoman Shirley Chisholm gave up her House of Representatives seat last year to focus on her personal priorities: her family and her grand piano, which she'd had little time for because of her pressing political commitments.

Even in the throes of his most stressful political years, former German chancellor Helmut Schmidt continued to record Mozart together with world-renowned pianists Christoph Eschenbach and Justus Frank. The latter noted, "I find professional pianists can seldom sight-read as well as Schmidt does."

Another pianist in office at this writing is Brazil's State Secretary of Culture, João Carlos Martins, who divides his time between his efforts to preserve national monuments and his concert tours and recordings. A Bach specialist, Martins is currently working to fulfill an enormous musical task: making an eighteen-disc record project of Bach's complete keyboard works in time for the composer's tricentennial in 1985.

The political situations in foreign countries have often hampered musical expression. Restrictions on classical—and indeed, all Western—music prevailed during the Cultural Revolution in China. Playing Mozart or Beethoven was even considered a

Ignaz Jan Paderewski

crime, and though pianists were not allowed to practice, they continued to do so, using their laps or the walls instead. Today, these restrictions are gone, and there's actually a passion for Western music in many Asian countries, especially in Japan and Korea.

Music's role in diplomacy is a decorative one, at best. But when New York Philharmonic conductor Zubin Mehta stepped forth and declared his world citizenship to the people of Buenos Aires, the response was deafening. During the orchestra's South American tour, Mehta made the decision to donate a concert to the Argentinian people after the Falkland Islands war in 1982. Mehta observed that music flies across national borders, hatred, and despair, reaching the hearts of people. He said, "As I was playing Beethoven, I was moved by a thought that the same kind of unity that goes into playing this kind of music goes into the unity that brings us together here today." A retired private secretary in the audience, who was interviewed by the press, perceptively added, "True artists fix all the harm that politicians do."

Pianist Jeffrey Kahane reflects that people criticized Beethoven's Ninth Symphony for setting up an unrealistic model of what life is like and for extolling seemingly unattainable notions of brotherhood and peace. "We *need* Beethoven's Ninth," contradicts Kahane, "to stand against Auschwitz, My Lai and the missiles everywhere around us. The human race has created this grave world situation of ours, and has also created Beethoven's Ninth Symphony."

THE PIANO GOES TO WAR

As the *Queen Elizabeth II* was making its way to the Falkland Islands in the spring of 1982, during Britain's conflict over the islands with Argentina, the crew actually dumped a Bösendorfer piano overboard to make room for helicopters to land on the ship!

- During the Vietnam War, a number of American prisoners held captive at what became known as the "Hanoi Hilton" refused to waste their time in captivity. Inventively, they fashioned their "Steinways" out of flat boards, with exact-size "keys" sketched in pencil. This enabled them to silently practice their favorite selections while in prison.
- Steinway pianos have occasionally been put on board submarines for a bit of deep-sea entertainment, and fared quite well despite the undersea pressure. One piano has been on a submarine for twenty years.

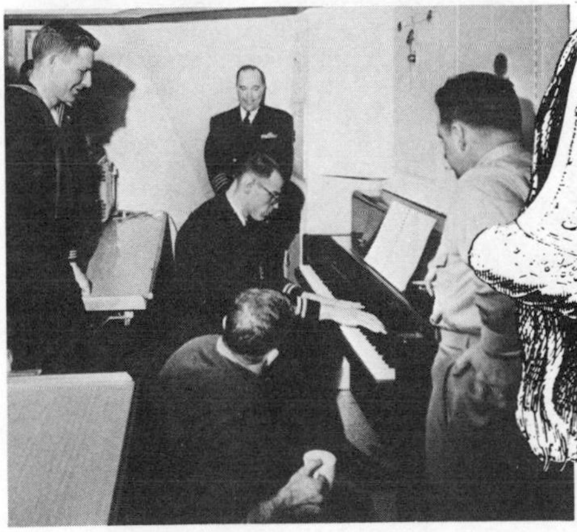

5

YOU AND THE PIANO WORLD

The Piano Knowledge Quiz

The Passion for the Piano Quiz that follows is designed to challenge your familiarity with piano lore. Answers begin on page 126.

1. The melodies of these popular songs were in many cases lifted from classical compositions note for note. Can you match each update with its source below?
   a. "I'm Always Chasing Rainbows"
   b. "The Lamp Is Low"
   c. "Tonight We Love"
   d. "A Groovy Kind of Love"
   e. "Could It Be Magic?"

   A. Ravel's "Pavane for a Dead Princess"
   B. Chopin's "Fantaisie-Impromptu"
   C. Tchaikovsky's First Piano Concerto
   D. Chopin's Prelude in C minor (op. 28, no. 20)
   E. Clementi's Sonatina no. 35

2. Which of these are piano touches?
   a. staccato
   b. allegro
   c. maestro
   d. rubato
   e. piano
   f. legato

3. The piano is the primary instrument for all of the following musicians, except for one. Who is it?
   a. Randy Newman
   b. Itzhak Perlman
   c. Lorin Hollander
   d. Vladimir Ashkenazy

4. With which features did Bartolommeo Cristofori replace the harpsichord plectra?
   a. axles
   b. strings
   c. hammers
   d. reeds

5. In which three Beatles songs was the piano prominent?
   a. "Michelle"
   b. "Let It Be"
   c. "Sgt. Pepper's Lonely Hearts Club Band"
   d. "Roll Over, Beethoven"
   e. "Hey Jude"
   f. "A Day in the Life"

6. Which former head of state was also a pianist?
   - **a. Charles de Gaulle**
   - **b. John F. Kennedy**
   - **c. Jan Ignaz Paderewski**
   - **d. Mao Zedong**

7. "Country Gardens" is a concert piano piece based on a modern folk song. Who wrote it?
   - **a. Percy Grainger**
   - **b. Edvard Grieg**
   - **c. Stephen Foster**
   - **d. Benjamin Britten**

8. These four bars of music are the beginning of
   - **a. Debussy's "Clair de Lune"**
   - **b. Schubert's "Marche Militaire"**
   - **c. Schumann's "Of Foreign Lands and People"**
   - **d. Beethoven's "Für Elise"**

9. In playing the piano "stride" style, you
   - **a. hit chords on the weak beats alternating with a bass note on the strong beats, left hand only**
   - **b. hit a bass note on the weak beats alternating with chords on the strong beats, left hand only**
   - **c. stride up and down the piano with both hands playing faster and louder until you reach fortissimo**
   - **d. play "boogie woogie" tunes in different modulations**

10. To whom did Beethoven dedicate his *Emperor* Piano Concerto?
    - **a. Julius Caesar**
    - **b. Napoleon**
    - **c. Franz Josef of Austria**
    - **d. no one in particular**

11. Of the following keyboard musicians, who was not featured on Miles Davis's influential jazz/rock album, *Bitches Brew*?
    - **a. Chick Corea**
    - **b. Joe Zawinul**
    - **c. Willie "The Lion" Smith**
    - **d. Herbie Hancock**

12. Identify this remarkable jazz and ragtime pianist with the long fingers.
    - **a. Duke Ellington**
    - **b. Thelonious Monk**
    - **c. Erroll Garner**
    - **d. Eubie Blake**

13. When Mozart needed a release from the stress in his life, he would
    a. **crawl around on all fours and play cat-and-mouse games**
    b. **jog in the Vienna woods**
    c. **open the window and threaten to jump**
    d. **write new melodies on his hands and feet**

14. "Chops" according to jazz and rock musicians are
    a. **chord changes**
    b. **technique**
    c. **money and material possessions**
    d. **none of the above**

15. Which of these four timely pieces of music was written for a piano and orchestra combination?
    a. ***Song Before Sunrise* (Delius)**
    b. ***Prelude to the Afternoon of a Faun* (Debussy)**
    c. ***Nights in the Gardens of Spain* (de Falla)**
    d. ***Night on Bald Mountain* (Moussorgsky)**

PIANO LORE

Duo piano teams usually have close musical relationships. But two French pianists, Marguerite Long and Alfred Cortot, couldn't stand each other and didn't exchange words for several years, though they performed as a duo. Instead, they had a middleman communicate between them and played together successfully for the French government for several years.

● Saloon keepers in the Old West put a sign above their barroom pianos to protect their entertainers' lives. It read: "Please don't shoot the piano player. He is doing his best."

● There were at least fifty-two musicians in the family of Johann Sebastian Bach. Bach himself never really took to the piano, having been brought up in the era of the harpsichord and clavichord. Although the newly invented piano was not easy for him to adjust to, several of his estimable sons were to compose for it. His youngest surviving son, Johann Christian, was to write piano sonatas in a style that influenced Mozart.

● At a New York concert given by the great eccentric pianist Vladimir de Pachmann, the pianist came out on stage reverently holding a pair of socks, which he kept on the piano during the performance. After the all-Chopin program, the music critics rushed backstage to pay their respects to the pianist. One senior critic asked de Pachmann about the socks. When de Pachmann solemnly replied that they had been worn one time by Frederic Chopin, the critic, overwhelmed, reached for the socks and reverently kissed them. Days later, de Pachmann was with some friends, who remarked about the historic occasion of such an important New York music critic kissing a pair of Chopin's socks. De Pachmann laughed and said, "They were not Chopin's socks. They were mine."

PIANO KEY

1. A–b; B–a; C–c; D–e; E–d.
2. a, f. Staccato indicates that you perform a note quickly and lightly, separating it from the notes before and after it. Legato means that you play without any perceptible interruption between the notes.
3. b. Perlman is a violinist.
4. c. Hammers took the piano on its own course—the strings were struck, not plucked as with past keyboard instruments.
5. b, e, f. Good for you, if you remembered all three! Although most rock groups of the sixties used the piano and keyboards only occasionally, the Beatles played them quite often.
6. c. Paderewski was the Premier of Poland in 1919, at the pinnacle of his concert career as a pianist. He also headed the Polish government in exile during the early years of the Second World War. As a pianist, he was second to none.
7. a. Most young piano students learn a simplified version of Percy Grainger's elaborate concert piece.
8. a. Nearly every piano student has played or attempted "Clair de Lune" (Moonlight).
9. a. "Stride" piano was named for the "striding" effect of the left hand playing in ten-key stretches.
10. d. Beethoven did not dedicate his great concerto to anyone. It was probably his publisher who did—dedications were a common practice at the time, to increase sales. Napoleon *had* at one time been Beethoven's hero, but the composer had become disillusioned with the emperor's thirst for a greater empire.
11. c. This Miles Davis "crossover" album was the meeting place of many great keyboard and other musicians. But Willie "The Lion" Smith, inventor of the Harlem Stride, was of an earlier generation.
12. d. Eubie was playing ragtime when it was first in vogue. He played the piano publicly till the age of 97, and was honored for his contribution to music shortly before his death, at 100.
13. a. One of the greatest geniuses the world has ever known would sometimes revert to childish play.
14. b. "Chops" was originally a jazz term, meaning a musician's hands, lips, or cheeks; by extension, it now also refers to the use musicians make of their natural equipment, that is, their ability to play, or, in classical terms, their technique.
15. c. *Nights in the Gardens of Spain* are symphonic impressions, but written for piano and orchestra. All the others are written purely for orchestra.

THOSE PIANO-LOVING ANIMALS

Two composers, living centuries apart, were both inspired by their pet cats to write pieces. When Domenico Scarlatti's cat struck certain notes on his harpsichord with its paws, Scarlatti proceeded to write "The Cat Fugue" for harpsichord. Similarly, while Chopin was composing Waltz no. 3 in F-Major, his cat stepped across the keys of the piano, amusing Chopin so much that he tried for the same sounds in what is called "The Cat's Waltz."

- A five-movement Sonata for Piano and Dog met with howling success recently when it was performed at a Carnegie Recital Hall concert and on television. Its Juilliard-trained composer, Kurt Nurock, says he's of the post–John Cage generation for whom "any sound can be musical." The Sonata is an elaborate 35-minute piece composed and performed by (human) pianist and sung by three dogs.

The Passion for the Piano Questionnaire

Pianists of all ages and stages usually have multitudes of memories, dreams, and hopes tied up with their instruments. Professional artists have such intimate relationships with their instruments that when they don't play for a week, some say, their fingers start to ache and they feel that something is missing from their lives. Often, they will talk about their "jealous Steinway," or their "demanding Bösendorfer." Even ex-pianists who haven't approached pianos since childhood still have powerful feelings about them, and will probably never forget their first piano lessons.

How's your relationship with the piano? Harmonious or discordant? Fiery or forgotten? This Passion for the Piano Questionnaire is designed for you to settle old scores or celebrate your relationship with the piano.

1. Your Present and Past Relationship with the Piano

A. Describe Your Relationship with the Piano Right Now

____ *Total ecstasy—I can't keep my hands off it*
____ *Very satisfying*
____ *Just friends*
____ *Can't live with the piano and can't live without it*
____ *We've separated*
____ *Haven't seen each other in years*
____ *Frustrating*
____ *Threatening*
____ *Piano? What piano?*

B. How Often and When Do You Play the Piano?

____ *I never let a day go by without playing it*
____ *I play several times a week*
____ *A couple of times a month*
____ *Only with other people*
____ *Only when I'm alone*
____ *When I'm in the mood*
____ *Only on special occasions (parties, Christmas, birthdays)*
____ *In moments of inspiration*
____ *I've never touched a piano in my life*
Other: ____________________

C. How Major or Minor is the Piano's Role in Your Life?

____ *I am a professional pianist*
____ *I play at parties*
____ *I'm a "Sunday" pianist*
____ *I teach piano*
____ *I accompany* __________
____ *I'm a piano student*
    ____ *Beginner*
    ____ *Intermediate*
    ____ *Advanced*
    ____ *Master Classes*
____ *I play by ear*
____ *I'd like to learn to play the piano*
____ *I just bought a piano*
____ *I'm thinking of starting lessons*
____ *I'm thinking of buying/renting a piano*
____ *I'm a former pianist. The last time I played one was* ____________
____ *I've toyed with the idea of going back to it*
____ *I'm a piano lover, not a piano player*
____ *I'm a distant admirer*
____ *There is no piano in my life*

D. Piano Lessons in My Life

Who of all your piano teachers most inspired you? Of your music teachers? What inspired you about them? Recall your piano past, and record your reminiscences.

E. Pianists I Have Heard

Recall the greatest piano performance you've ever heard. Has there been a pianist whose style you hope to emulate?

F. How Do You Feel Your Piano Regards You?

Mentally step away from the keyboard for a moment and try to get an idea of how your piano feels being played by you. (Or not be-

ing played by you, if that's the case.) From the piano's standpoint, could your touch be more pleasing? You might want to consider how your particular piano reacts to your type of music. Is it waiting for you to play some jazz on it?

2. Your Secret Piano Fantasies

Some classical pianists say they dream of playing jazz one day, and cocktail pianists long to play Brahms. Here's an opportunity to indulge in your own fantasies and reveal your secret piano ambition. Check off the fantasies that apply.

____ *To play a Liszt-Paganini étude and dazzle everybody*
____ *To play cocktail piano at Michael's Pub in New York City*
____ *To join Devo*
____ *To play chamber music at Tanglewood or the Aspen Music Festival*

____ *To play on the* Queen Elizabeth II
____ *To accompany the Joffrey Ballet*
____ *To play a solo with the Philadelphia Orchestra*
____ *To accompany Pavarotti or Domingo*
____ *To become the star on your block by playing in the local hall and having the whole neighborhood acclaim your genius*
____ *To celebrate the holiday spirit on the piano*
____ *To demonstrate Baldwin pianos on Saturdays in shopping center malls*
____ *To play Chopin's "Minute Waltz" in fifty seconds*
____ *To have them hanging from the chandeliers when you play Liszt's "La Campanella"*
____ *To play the Tchaikovsky concerto in the competition in Moscow*
____ *To be proclaimed the "second Van Cliburn," and win the competition*
____ *To cut an LP record*
____ *To have it be a hit*
____ *To have lunch with André Watts*
____ *To discover a new piano technique that makes practicing unnecessary*
____ *To have as much fun and flair as Liberace*
____ *To have a Horowitz technique and assure people it comes naturally*
____ *To appear on local television stations as a featured pianist*
____ *To earn $100,000 a year as a pianist*
____ *To appear at the Kool Jazz Festival as the major piano soloist*
____ *To win the Nobel Prize for your contribution to music*
____ *To practice your keyboard harmony with a Russian pianist and bring about a nuclear freeze*

Multiply by four every piano fantasy you've checked off to see how passionate your passion for the piano really is.

PASSION FOR THE PIANO RATING

80 to 100	Your passion knows no bounds.
50 to 80	Let yourself go and you'll move right up the scale to full passion.
20 to 50	Buy some new music or write your own. Increase your playing by 50 percent and don't stop till the flames are crackling.
0 to 20	Buy a piano T-shirt and start taking piano lessons.

Music Schools and Conservatories

There was a time when young American musicians would run off at the drop of a hat to study at the conservatories in Paris or Vienna, where, it was felt, the training excelled. Now, top-notch American conservatories and university music schools and departments are attracting talent from all over the world. The piano departments in these institutions have grown in stature over the last twenty-five years, drawing faculties of indisputable rank. Even neighborhood music schools, many of which were originally settlement houses, have become significant musical training grounds.

Conservatories which used to offer essentially performance programs now insist on academic courses as well, although they are still geared for performers. Most conservatories today also have university affiliations. The noted Eastman School of Music, for example, is part of the University of Rochester. There are, however, notable exceptions: the Juilliard School, the Manhattan School of Music, and the New England Conservatory of Music are all privately endowed. In Europe, conservatories such as the famous Vienna and Munich Conservatories are state-supported, making for a very reasonably priced education.

A university or a college will have either a music department or a school of music. Music departments generally offer courses in theory, composition, sight-singing (or solfeggio), musicology, and analysis, in addition to any instrumental instruction. In some departments, students can major in performance, musicology, or composition. A school of music is larger than a music department, geared more toward performance, and representative of more diverse musical fields such as musicology, theory, performance, composition, and pedagogy (how to teach). A school of music is quite independent from the university or college and is often considered a professional school within a university.

The term "music school" is commonly applied to conservatories such as Juilliard or to neighborhood schools. A music school offers practical instruction at all levels. Hence, the universal image of a child bearing a violin case or flute case, or a pianist with sheet music, en route to a lesson.

Nine of the most important conservatories are described below in alphabetical order, followed by a general list of excellent music schools, departments, colleges, and conservatories. If you are interested in a specific curriculum or conservatory, you may want to consult music directories, in particular *Musical America*.

Berklee College of Music (1140 Boylston Street, Boston, MA 02215). Berklee is known nationwide for its strong jazz, rock, and pop orientation. Twenty-six hundred undergraduates attend, including 400 foreign students from sixty-six countries. One of the largest colleges of music in the world, it is proud of its electronic synthesizer laboratory, which provides hands-on training in synthesizer performance and composing techniques. Other courses include jazz composition, film scoring, electronic music, "The Music of John Lennon," "The Piano in the Rhythm Section," and "Jazz Arranging for Large Ensembles." Traditional courses in voicing, piano literature, and transposing are also given. Famous alumni include Keith Jarrett, Jan Hammer, Quincy Jones, and Joe Zawinul.

Curtis Institute of Music (1726 Locust Street, Philadelphia, PA 19103). A very fine, old, Eastern conservatory, and one of the most élite. Admission only by audition; accepts 100 students per class. Has a four-year program leading to a diploma degree. Once accepted, every student receives a full scholarship (which is how Juilliard used to be years ago). Jorge Bolet heads the piano department. A totally classical-oriented school. Courses in instruments, accompanying, voice, theory, counterpoint, techniques of twentieth-century music. Also has a high school program. No specific time limit for any level: you can come at any age and stay as long as it takes to complete your program of study.

Eastman School of Music (26 Gibbs Street, Rochester, NY 14604). Offers degrees to 650 students all told in performing, musicology, composition, and education. A very well-established school; in fact, it's almost better known than the very fine, large university of which it is a part (the University of Rochester).

The Juilliard School (Lincoln Center Plaza, New York, NY 10023). This is the best-known conservatory in America. It offers top training in music, theater, and dance. Nine hundred and twenty-five students from all parts of the world are taught by a 200-member faculty of international renown. Piano teachers include Adele Marcus, Rudolf Firkusny, and Sasha Gorodnitzki. Over ninety percent of Juilliard's graduates find jobs in their fields. Although this is primarily a performance school, classes are taught in the history and analysis of piano music, and so forth. Juilliard alumni include Van Cliburn, Itzhak Perlman, Marvin Hamlisch, Byron Janis, and Misha Dichter.

Manhattan School of Music (120 Claremont Avenue, New York, NY 10027). The largest private conservatory in America, Manhattan has a strong piano department, an energetic faculty, and an adventurous curriculum. It offers everything from Baroque specialist Rosalyn Tureck's Bach Institute to jazz improvisation courses and electronic music performance and composition. Manhattan has developed over the years from a neighborhood music school into a major conservatory rivaling Juilliard (it occupies Juilliard's old building). Its distinguished piano faculty includes John Browning, Constance Keene, Dora Zaslavsky, Gary Graffman, and Seymour Lipkin, with master classes by visitors such as André Watts. Courses include piano, sight-reading, theory, pop/rock/jazz harmony, writing for film and television, piano teaching, and piano repair. Six hundred eighty-one students are enrolled at the school, which also has a large preparatory department for children and less advanced students, as well as an extension division.

Mannes College of Music (157 East 74th Street, New York, NY 10028). A fine four-year private conservatory with a preparatory division. The top-notch piano faculty includes Peter Serkin, Richard Goode, Claude Frank, and Edith Oppens. Low profile/high caliber school located in Manhattan. Classes in keyboard harmony, jazz piano, and so on.

New England Conservatory of Music (290 Huntington Avenue, Boston, MA 07115). A fine conservatory offering both traditional and contemporary music courses in blues, piano techniques, sonata playing, instrumental accompaniment, piano tuning and repair, and techniques of playing twentieth-century music. Seven hundred twenty students, 150 faculty.

Oberlin Conservatory of Music, Oberlin College (Oberlin, OH 44074). One of the oldest and finest conservatories in America, the Oberlin Conservatory is located thirty-five miles outside Cleveland and offers courses ranging from opera and symphonic music to jazz ensemble and electronic music. Oberlin can assure students it has enough pianos—300, 180 of which are Steinways. The conservatory offers degrees in music, theater, teaching, and conducting.

Peabody Conservatory, Johns Hopkins University (1 East Mt. Vernon Place, Baltimore, MD 21202). Performance oriented, but also gives a degree in music education. Now has a recording arts and sciences major, in conjunction with Johns Hopkins. Five hundred students in undergraduate and graduate programs. Distinguished faculty includes Leon Fleisher and Walter Haupzig.

OTHER MUSIC SCHOOLS AND CONSERVATORIES IN THE UNITED STATES AND ABROAD

The Banff School of Fine Arts (Banff, Alberta, Canada). A summer school until recently, Banff is now a year-round operation with master classes in piano and coaching in strings/piano and voice/piano. The fine faculty includes Menahem Pressler, Jorge Mester, and Barry Tuckwell.

Cal Arts (California Institute of the Arts) (Valencia, CA). The unusual curriculum includes courses in Indian, Indonesian, and African music and dance. Its school of music has 160 students and offers degrees in performance, composition, and general music.

Cincinnati Conservatory, The University of Cincinnati's College Conservatory of Music (Cincinnati, OH). A distinguished conservatory for music, theater, and dance. Teaches all aspects of music.

City College of New York (New York, NY). A generalized music department, with 150 students, that is unique in being one of the only full-fledged jazz and pop programs on the East Coast. Musicians can study at the music department, or at the new Davis Center for the Performing Arts, at which one can earn a Bachelor of Fine Arts from City College. City College also has a graduate program. John Lewis, of the Modern Jazz Quartet, is on the faculty of City College.

Cleveland Institute of Music (Cleveland, OH). Courses in performance, composition, theory, and eurythmics (body movement in relation to music). Its president is pianist Grant Johannesen.

Converse College School of Music (Spartanburg, SC). This professional school of music has been in existence since 1889, and offers across-the-board programs in performance, theory, composition, musicology, music education, and piano pedagogy. Has a unique relationship with the Brevard Music Center in North Carolina, a summer music camp and festival for people between twelve and thirty, and offers college credit for courses taken at Brevard.

The Fontainebleau School of Music (Fontainebleau, France). Located in a French palace outside of Paris. Excellent professional training; many distinguished American graduates, such as Aaron Copland. The school was developed by Nadia Boulanger, considered one of the most influential teachers of music—specifically, the piano—in the twentieth century.

Harvard University (Cambridge, MA). Harvard's music department is the oldest in America and has been attended by Leonard Bernstein, Elliott Carter, and "new music" proponents such as Ursula Oppens. Seventy-five students study music, musicology, and composition.

Indiana University, School of Music (Bloomington, IN). This is the largest, and, many say, the finest university music school. It is definitely performance oriented, with five full orchestras, three bands, choral and instrumental ensembles, jazz and electronic music ensembles, full-scale ballet productions, and chamber music. Seventeen hundred students attend the School of Music, which has a faculty of 140. A wide range of courses is offered, from classical to jazz piano, music history of all periods, and electronic music. Indiana is competitive, but as one professor admitted, "If you can't take the competition here, you can't take it outside school." The school presents 1000 on-campus musical performances each year.

Miami University, School of Music (Miami, Florida). The largest private school of music attached to a private university, Miami also has the largest program of music courses in the world; it offers ten different undergraduate degrees, thirty-two graduate degrees, and several first-of-their-kind majors, including music engineering technology and music merchandising (music in business). Eight hundred students attend this noted progressive school. Strong in music courses, classical and jazz piano.

Munich Conservatory (Hochschule für Musik) (Munich, Germany). World-renowned, it was founded in 1846 and reorganized according to Richard Wagner's specifications. It offers theory, composition, and piano, and is one of the largest schools in Germany.

Northwestern University, School of Music (Evanston, IL). Degrees in church music, music history, literature, and education.

Queens College, the Aaron Copland School of Music (Queens, NY). The musical "jewel" of the New York City colleges. Emphasis is on theory, musicology, composition, and performing. Named in the composer's honor; recently expanded to a school of music with 300 students. Courses are offered in theory, harmony, counterpoint, applied keyboard skills, analysis, orchestration. A cultural oasis, it also has a preparatory school since there is no conservatory training available in Queens or on Long Island, where the Aaron Copland School is located.

Paris Conservatory (Conservatoire National Supérieur de Musique) (Paris, France). An internationally famous conservatory, founded in 1795. Nine divisions, including classes in composition, music theory and piano and harp instruction.

Philadelphia College of the Performing Arts (Philadelphia, PA). Many members of the Philadelphia Orchestra teach here. Degrees in music and opera are offered.

Rice University, The Shepherd School of Music (Houston, TX). An up-and-coming school for "young artists and scholars who want to pursue performing careers in music." Offers degrees in performance, theory, composition, and music history.

Royal Academy of Music (London, England). One of the oldest institutions for advanced musical training in Europe, the 675-student Academy offers programs in performance and theoretical music studies.

Royal College of Music (London, England). Like the Royal Academy, the Royal College is an international conservatory offering performing and academic programs.

San Francisco Conservatory (San Francisco, CA). A four-year up-and-coming college of music. Part of the cultural renaissance of the San Francisco Bay Area. The only accredited music school west of the Mississippi, the conservatory has a reputation for humaneness, and prides itself on its close-knit, supportive environment. Offers degrees in performing and composition. Two hundred students, forty faculty. Has a special relationship with the Shanghai Conservatory in mainland China, and has trained some of their most gifted aspiring pianists.

University of California at Berkeley, Music Department (Berkeley, CA). In a recent national survey, Berkeley was in first place in faculty and tied for first place in graduate music departments with Princeton and Chicago. Emphasis here is on musicology and harmony rather than on performing. One hundred and twenty-five students. Faculty includes Joseph Kerman, Andrew Imbrie, and Alan Curtis.

University of California at Los Angeles (Los Angeles, CA). The music school is housed in Schoenberg Hall (the composer Arnold Schoenberg was on its faculty). It is a classical-oriented school, with fine faculty such as Aube Tzerko and pianist Johana Harris (who is married to composer Roy Harris). Student-teacher ratio of almost four to one. Emphasis here is on performance, but the school is also strong in musicology, ethnomusicology, composition, and music education.

University of Redlands, School of Music (Redlands, CA). A performing school of music within a small, selective liberal arts university that was established in 1907. Offers bachelor's and master's degrees in church music, performance, accompanying, coaching, and composition.

University of New Mexico, Department of Music (Albuquerque, NM). Offers bachelor's and master's degrees; outstanding faculty of artist-teachers.

University of Southern California, School of Music (University Park, Los Angeles, CA). This is a fine example of an outstanding school of music within a large university. Musicians such as Jascha Heifetz and Igor Piatigorsky taught at USC for many years, and John Perry and other piano pedagogues are currently on the faculty. Whereas most schools have piano departments, USC has a keyboard department, because they feel it covers more territory. Students learn solo and chamber music, plus accompaniment and pedagogy. A keyboard department spokesman said that the purpose of this diversified preparation is "to train our very good performers for a realistic position in today's musical world." There are 700 students in undergraduate and graduate programs, and a faculty of 125. Famous USC alumni include conductor Michael Tilson Thomas, singer Marilyn Horne, and jazzman Herb Alpert.

Vienna Conservatory (Hochschule für Musik) (Vienna, Austria). Located next door to the Vienna Konzerthaus Building. Faculty includes many teaching musicians from the opera and from the Vienna Philharmonic. One of the great European conservatories.

Yale University, School of Music (New Haven, CT). This school of music is second to none. Its undergraduate and graduate programs offer degrees in performance and composition. Three-to-one ratio of students to teacher. Master classes by famous visiting composers and performers. Claude Frank is on the piano faculty, and John Mehegan, the jazz pianist and educator, teaches theory and musicianship. One thousand recitals and concerts are offered at Yale each year.

Places to Go, People to Hear, Music to Buy

Pianists may be composing, creating, and playing the piano all over town—piano bars, restaurants, clubs and concert halls—but their music is available in selective spots—music and book stores, libraries, conservatories, and electronics companies. By far, the most accessible of these are the music stores, which carry sheet music, instruments, accessories, books, magazines, concert tickets, and paraphernalia ranging from Mozart T-shirts to music-motif tote bags.

Pianists and other musicians who work in music stores can be veritable music encyclopedias; they may be able to help you unearth the right edition or version of a piece, and may also offer advice on which editions have the best fingering, most dynamic markings, best phrasing, and lowest prices. Also ask for secondhand sheet music. One Juilliard student found a collection of Scarlatti sonatas, in an excellent

edition published by Ricordi of Italy, on sale at a music store for two dollars—one-eighth of the going price. As I was searching for a recording of Beethoven's *Appassionata* Sonata no. 23 in F-minor, the attending salesperson turned out to be a musical expert. He ran down a list of twenty or so Beethoven interpreters and selected one pianist we both liked. This pianist, however, had recorded the sonata on two different albums with other sonatas. Looking at one of them, the salesperson remarked in disgust: "What a poor programming idea—putting three Beethoven sonatas that are all in minor keys onto the same album!" I saw his point immediately, and took the other album.

Don't let what happened to one young music lover become your record fate. After purchasing her first Chopin album, played by an unknown pianist with a long German name, she rushed home to play it, and, to her dismay, she could barely recognize the tempi and dynamics of her favorite Chopin preludes and études. Later she was informed that she would have been safe with any recording by Artur Rubinstein, Vladimir Horowitz, or Dinu Lipatti. Also, albums made at different periods in a pianist's life can vary widely. In jazz, for example, the pianist-composer may take a totally different musical direction, changing bands, styles, and sometimes even keyboard instruments.

A HANDFUL OF TOP MUSIC STORES IN THE UNITED STATES AND EUROPE

Boston, MA. Boston Music Company, 116 Boylston Street. The largest music store in New England. Offers classical, jazz, improvisation, and ragtime books. Sheet music includes classical scores and popular songs. Mail order.

Bryn Mawr, PA. Theodore Press Publishers, Presser Place. Extensive piano sheet music. Mail order.

Chicago, IL. Carl Fischer Publishers, 312 South Wabash Ave. Music publishers, also located in Boston, Los Angeles, and New York. Mail order.

Cincinnati, OH. Willis Music Co. Four retail stores, including 7th and Race streets.

Copenhagen, Denmark. Wilhelm Hansen, Gothersgade 9–11. One of the oldest music publishers in Northern Europe. Has a shop in the heart of Copenhagen where you can buy scores and sheet music and tickets for performances and events.

London, England. Chimes Music Shop, 65 Marylebone High Street, London W1. Located by the Royal Academy of Music. A useful source of scores and sheet music.

Minneapolis, MN. Schmitt Music Centers, 88 South Tenth Street (800) 328-8480. The Midwest's largest music store, and one of the largest nationwide. Takes phone orders for sheet music and piano methods. In fact, the Schmitt salespeople are so knowledgeable that if you can hum a tune for a piece whose name you don't remember,

the clerk can usually identify it and order it for you. Schmitt also sponsors piano workshops, clinics, and weekly piano teachers' meetings.

New York, NY. Schirmer Music, 40 West 62nd Street, is one of the most prestigious music publishers in America. Located close to Lincoln Center and the Juilliard School. Has a huge printed music collection and also carries books, records, and music accessories.

New York, NY. Joseph Patelson Music House, 160 West 56th Street. Opposite the stage entrance to Carnegie Hall. It stocks mostly classical, but also has scores of contemporary favorites and a good selection of books on music. Well-known to pianists.

Paris, France. Durand & Fils, 4 rue de la Madeleine. A well-established French music publisher with an excellent Debussy—and other French composers—piano music section.

Salt Lake City, UT. Daynes Music Co., 156 South Main Street. A major music haven for the West carrying new and used pianos and organs, as well as sheet music.

San Francisco, CA. Pacific Coast Music, 141 Kearny Street. Large store and distributor for Hansen House Music of popular sheet music (rock and jazz). Ships to Australia, Los Angeles, and the Midwest. Also sells portable keyboards: Casio and Yamaha. Pianos—new and used—are sold upstairs at Sherman Clay.

MUSIC FESTIVALS

The music festivals held around the world every summer can heighten a music lover's life. Festival performances are often more inspired than those given during a regular season. The relaxed mood, altered pace, and the beauty or uniqueness of the location stimulates the players and audience alike.

In the last decade, music festivals have proliferated in America and worldwide to become a source of exciting musical experience for millions of people. Audiences benefit from high quality, low ticket prices, and extensive, adventurous musical programming.

Described below are several important summer music festivals known for their caliber of performers, programs, and festival atmosphere.

The Aspen Music Festival (June through August). Against a ski-country backdrop, this festival offers a tremendous variety of musical activities, from chamber music concerts to large-scale opera and orchestral performances. Master piano classes with well-known piano artists such as Misha Dichter and Claude Frank are offered at the Aspen Music School, which runs concurrently with the festival. World-famous pianists are on the festival board, and performers, teachers, students, and, in some cases, audiences come from all over the world. For information, contact the Aspen Music School and Festival, Box AA, Aspen, CO 81612, (303) 925-3524.

The Kool Jazz Festival (June through August). The old Newport Jazz Festival has now mushroomed into a twenty-city festival taking place every year in major American cities from Atlanta to Seattle. It presents the very best jazz and soul performers, from Oscar Peterson to Ella Fitzgerald to Chick Corea. Traditional groups such as Dave Brubeck and the Modern Jazz Quartet perform alongside avant-garde groups such as Spyro Gyra. Ninety-six thousand people—more than ever before—attended the Kool Jazz Festival in 1982. Contact the Kool Jazz Festival at its headquarters: 311 West 74th Street, New York, NY 10023, (212) 873-0733.

Tanglewood (July through August). Its official name is the Berkshire Music Festival, but it is known to everyone as "Tanglewood," the summer home of the Boston Symphony Orchestra. In addition to the twenty-four regular concerts given by the Boston Symphony, there are weekly "Prelude" concerts, open rehearsals, recitals, chamber music, an annual festival of contemporary music, and concerts almost daily by the young musicians who are Fellows of the Berkshire Music Center. About 300,000 people usually attend this eight-week festival. In 1982, soloists included pianists Alfred Brendel, Emanuel Ax, Ken Noda, and Peter Serkin. At Tanglewood you may hear conductors such as Leonard Bernstein, Seiji Ozawa, Luciano Berio, or André Previn. Information is available from: Tanglewood, Lenox, MA 01240, (617) 266-1492 during summer months. Otherwise, write c/o Boston Symphony, Boston, MA 02115.

Mostly Mozart (July and August). Performances are given in New York City, and there are also limited engagements in Washington, D.C., and San Francisco. The predominantly classical programs are played by chamber

Teddy Wilson on piano and Benny Goodman on clarinet

Tanglewood

Dave Brubeck at Newport Jazz Festival

musicians and small ensembles. The price of admission enables you to hear a "preconcert recital"—a mini-performance before the regular program—making this two concerts for the price of one. Previous performers have included Alicia de Larrocha, Alexis Weissenberg, and André-Michel Schub. (Perhaps you've already seen the "Mostly Mozart" coffee mugs, T-shirts and candies.) Contact: "Mostly Mozart," c/o Lincoln Center for the Performing Arts, 140 West 65th Street, New York, NY 10023, (212) 874-2424.

Other excellent summer music festivals, in the United States and abroad, are listed below.

Aix-en-Provence Festival (Aix-en-Provence, France). One of France's oldest festivals. Concerts given in courtyards of medieval and eighteenth-century buildings. Classical music.

Bath Festival (Bath, England). Offers a delicious range of musical activities, as well as the opportunity to enjoy the celebrated waters. Known for the promotion of music by contemporary composers.

Berlin Festival (Berlin, Germany). Held in the Berlin Opera House and in halls and theaters throughout the city. Classical, opera, orchestral, many piano soloists.

Bregenz Festival (Bregenz, Austria). Classical-oriented; major soloists such as Wilhelm Kempff, Jorge Demus.

Brigham Young University Summer Piano Festival (& Gina Bachauer International Piano Competition) (Provo, UT). Classical music. Piano artists such as Grant Johannesen.

Caramoor Festival (Katonah, NY). Piano recitals, ensemble, opera, vocal, and orchestral performances. The festival is located fifty miles north of New York City. Offers classical music, with artists such as Alicia de Larrocha, Rudolf Firkusny, and John Browning having performed in the past.

Chicago Festival (Chicago, IL). Jazz, blues, rock, classical, pop, country.

Dubrovnik Summer Festival (Dubrovnik, Yugoslavia). Over one thousand performances, including piano concertos, orchestral concerts, and ballet.

Edinburgh International Festival (Edinburgh, Scotland). Renowned European festival; offers world premieres. Alicia de Larrocha has performed here. Classical.

Festival of Flanders. Held in various locations throughout Belgium, including Brussels, Bruges, Ghent, and Antwerp. One of Europe's most diverse festivals—operas, ensemble groups, soloists, and orchestras perform here from all over the world.

Grand Teton Music Festival (Teton Village, WY). One hundred artists, including concertmasters and gold medalists of international competitions, play at this festival, held in a national park. Classical music.

Greek Theater (Griffith Park, Los Angeles, CA). Pop, jazz, rock 'n' roll, folk, soul, country, rhythm and blues.

Hollywood Bowl Summer Festival (Los Angeles, CA). Pop pianists, among many other musicians, give open-air performances.

Interlochen Arts Festival (Interlochen, MI). Classical. Also the home of the National Music Camp—the "daddy" of music camps.

Jazz Parade of Nice (Nice, France). "Le jazz hot" wafts from the amphitheater of the Cimiez Gardens. Performers have included Gato Barbieri and Dave Brubeck.

Monster concerts were the brainchild of Louis Moreau Gottschalk, internationally famous nineteenth-century pianist and America's first national composer. Gottschalk loved to put on monster concerts with as many orchestras, choruses, bands, and pianos as possible—there were sometimes 900 musicians in all. At one concert in Argentina, fifty-six pianists and two orchestras played together. Pianist Eugene List revived the monster concert concept in the 1970s and '80s. Like Gottschalk, List felt they provided a great deal of fun and an opportunity for many pianists to perform together. At a recent monster concert there were forty-two pianists in all; at most, twenty pianists at ten pianos played at the same time.

Gottschalk's first monster concert

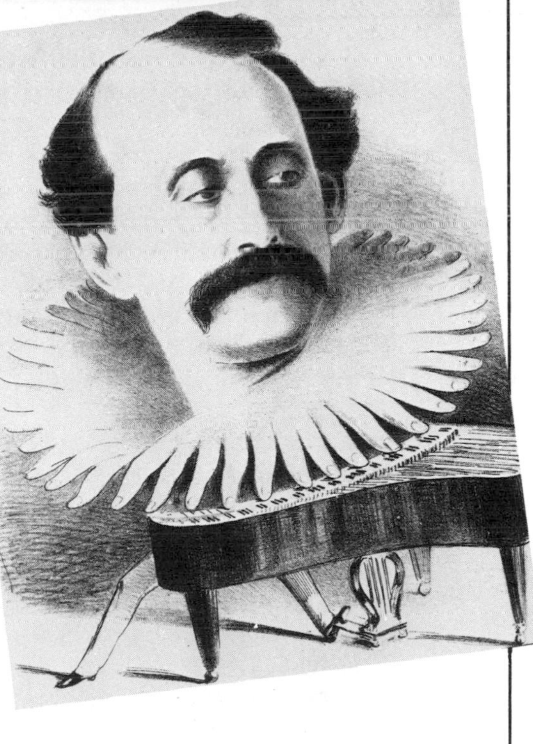

Carnegie Hall concert, 1979

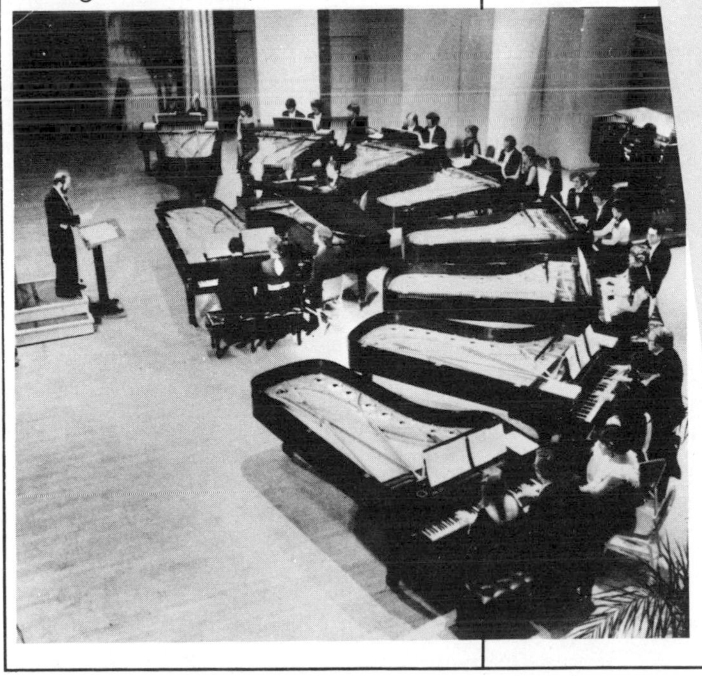

Leeds Music Festival (Leeds, England). Choral, orchestral, and chamber music. Classical.

Marlboro Music Festival (Marlboro, VT). Noted classical festival; also a training ground for soloists and chamber musicians. Rudolf Serkin is the director.

Monterey Jazz Festival (Monterey, CA). Established in 1958. Jazz and pop performers in the past have included John Lewis, Dizzy Gillespie, Lionel Hampton.

Montreux International Jazz Festival (Montreux, Switzerland). Attracts top jazz performers from all over, such as Ray Charles and Oscar Peterson. Offers a kaleidoscope of styles and performances. Most concerts take place in the Montreux Casino on the shore of Lake Geneva.

Moscow Music Summer (Moscow, U.S.S.R.). A classical and pop festival (there's also a spring festival in Leningrad, that has opera and ballet).

Music at the Vineyards (Paul Masson Vineyards, Saratoga, CA). Classical chamber music in lush surroundings.

New Orleans Jazz and Heritage Festival (New Orleans, LA). Emphasis on jazz, traditional, and Dixieland. Also rhythm and blues, gospel, Cajun, country. More interesting than Mardi Gras, natives say.

New World Festival of the Arts (Miami, FL). Jazz, classical, opera, dance, mime. One of our newest festivals—opened in 1982.

Osaka Festival (Osaka, Japan). An important musical and artistic festival, featuring the 'Noh' Japanese theater as well as Western soloists such as pianist Alexis Weissenberg.

Ravinia Festival (Highland Park, IL). Classical festival. Summer home of Chicago Symphony; features many piano soloists.

Romantic Festival of Nohant (Fêtes Romantiques de Nohant) (La

Châtre, France). An exciting two-week festival held in a barn on the estate of the Château Georges Sand at Nohant. Soloists have included Claudio Arrau and Michel Béroff.

Salzburg Festival (Salzburg, Austria). One of the major music events in Europe for the last fifty years. Plenty of Mozart (who was born here) and other classical music. Herbert von Karajan is the honored conductor. Orchestral performances, and solo recitals have been by Maurizio Pollini and Claudio Arrau.

Santa Fe Chamber Music Festival (Sante Fe, NM; also travels to San Diego and Seattle). Important American composers, such as Aaron Copland and William Schuman, are in residence here.

Spoleto Festival of Two Worlds (Spoleto, Italy). Dance spectaculars, plays, operas, and soloists.

Spoleto Festival USA (Charleston, SC). The American counterpart of the Italian Spoleto Festival. Classical music and a variety of dance, theater, opera, and ensemble (mini-concerts) performances.

Vienna Festival (Vienna, Austria). An all-encompassing festival. This musical city offers 1000 different performances, with famous conductors, instrumentalists, and singers from all over the world.

Wichita Jazz Festival (Wichita, KS). Jazz, bluegrass, symphonic music, Dixieland.

Wolf Trap Farm for the Performing Arts (Vienna, VA). The 1982 season closed with a festival of piano concertos played by André Watts, André-Michel Schub, and Horacio Gutierrez. Symphony, chamber, opera, folk, jazz, country, dance, mime and puppet shows.

CONCERT HALLS AND AUDITORIUMS

One of the most obvious places to go to hear pianists is a concert hall or auditorium. Following is a selected listing of worldwide concert "emporiums"—and of the (proverbial) piano bars.

Amsterdam, Netherlands. Concertgebouw (Concert Hall), Von Baerlestraat, 98. Home of the Concertgebouw Orchestra, plus chamber orchestra, choirs, and solo concerts.

Albuquerque, NM. Popejoy Concert Hall, University of New Mexico. Solo instrumentalists, ensemble, and orchestra.

Boston, MA. Symphony Hall, 300 Massachusetts Avenue. Has youth concerts and open rehearsals as well as all the expected major piano virtuosi and symphonic performances.

Bozeman, MT. Montana State University Performing Arts Series at Ellen Theatre, 17 West Main Street. Piano recitals, opera, ballet, and chamber music.

Chicago, IL. Georg Solti Orchestra Hall, 220 South Michigan Ave. Major soloists, as well as every conceivable ensemble group, and, of course, the Chicago Symphony.

Dallas, TX. Fair Park Music Hall, 1st and Parry streets. Classical, pop, rock, and jazz with performers from Joel Grey to Bella Davidovich.

Kalamazoo, MI. Miller Auditorium, Vandegissen Road. The *Nutcracker Suite* ballet and plenty of piano concertos.

London, England. Barbican Center, London EC2Y 8DS. New home of the London Symphony Orchestra and other classical performers.

Los Angeles, CA. Dorothy Chandler Pavilion. All the major soloists, European and American, play here, at the home of the Los Angeles Philharmonic. Or proceed to UCLA's fine Royce or Schoenberg halls, where there are plenty of dance and theater groups as well.

Memphis, TN. Vincent de Frank Music Hall, 3100 Walnut Grove. Part of the touring circuit of classical musicians, along with the Memphis Symphony Orchestra and other Tennessee talents.

New York, NY. Carnegie Hall, 881 Seventh Avenue. Piano virtuosi, orchestras, ballets, soloists, and chamber musicians from all over the world.

New York, NY. Alice Tully Hall at Lincoln Center. Primarily for piano recitals and chamber ensembles.

New York, NY. The Metropolitan Museum of Art, 81st Street and Fifth Avenue. Has "Great Pianists" series.

New York, NY. The Ritz, 119 East 11th Street. Popular rock/new wave club downtown; all the latest rock bands, with flashy keyboards and players.

Paris, France. Palais des Congrès, 2 Place de la Porte Maillot, Paris 75017. Besides orchestral concerts conducted by Daniel Barenboim, you can hear popular concerts as well.

Phoenix, AZ. Symphony Hall, 6328 North 7th Street. Music from A

Davies Hall, San Francisco

to Z—that is, from Lorin Hollander to Henry Mancini.

Pittsburgh, PA. Heinz Hall, 600 Penn Avenue. Soloists of caliber appear with the Pittsburgh Symphony Orchestra, conducted by André Previn. Also, you'll find a "Tiny Tots & Little People's Series," American Composers Forum, and Great Performers Series.

San Francisco, CA. Louise Davies Symphony Hall, 201 Van Ness. An ultramodern design. Pianists, ensembles, choruses, and orchestra.

San Francisco, CA. Keystone Korner, 750 Vallejo Street. The latest and greatest in rock/pop/new wave/ blues entertainment.

Tokyo, Japan. Toranomon (classical concert hall), 3-2-3 Kasumigaseki, Chiyoda-ku, Tokyo 100. Most major international classical pianists and other artists perform here.

Nakano Sun Plaza, 4-1-1 Nakano, Nakano-ku, Tokyo 164. Pop groups and performers such as Elton John and Cat Stevens.

Toronto, Canada. Town Hall & Theatre, St. Lawrence Centre. Name pianists and other important artists, playing everything from early music (pre-1600) to music by the Swingle Singers.

Washington, D.C. Kennedy Center for the Performing Arts, 2700 F Street N.W. Mstislav Rostropovich conducts the National Symphony, often with piano concerto guest artists, at the Concert Hall. The Kennedy Center Terrace Theater has smaller music groups, as well as dance and mime.

PIANO BARS

ATLANTA

Moonshadow Saloon, 1880 Johnson Road. Six hundred fifty people at a time can listen to live bands playing all kinds of music, from country to rock and jazz.

Country Place at Colony Square Complex, 1197 Peachtree Street. Dining pleasure is accentuated here by a nightly pianist who plays jazz and standard "mellow" piano music; big bands at holiday time.

BALTIMORE

The Brass Elephant, 924 North Charles Street. A jazz pianist plays at cocktail hour and again on weekend nights in this superb wine bar that has a crystal chandelier.

BOSTON

Jason's, 131 Clarendon Street. A popular Boston bar and nightclub, where the piano bar and a gourmet deli share the upstairs.

Montana's, 160 Commonwealth Avenue. Local, very accomplished bands play live jazz in a sophisticated, cozy piano bar atmosphere, art deco style.

CHICAGO

Biddy Mulligan's, 7644 North Sheridan. Offers great Chicago blues artists most weekends, and, once a month, ska, reggae, and punk.

B.L.U.E.S., 2519 North Halsted. A small neighborhood spot that offers great blues every night with musicians such as Sunnyland Slim, "the great piano ace."

Rick's Café Américain (Holiday Inn Lakeshore), East Ontario Street at North Lake Shore Drive. A very "Casablanca"-type environment; fine jazz artists.

The Pump Room, Ambassador East Hotel, 1301 North State Parkway. In this formal, historic room, Nat King Cole's pianist brother Ike plays in a low-key style.

CINCINNATI

Arnold's Bar & Grill, 210 East Eighth Street. An eclectic neighborhood bar with good live music that is as varied as the patrons: traditional, folk, jazz, and ragtime music.

DALLAS

Nick's Uptown, 3606 Greenville. Superior music, with prominent entertainers appearing nightly in concert format.

The Saloon, 2818 Greenville. Headquarters for acoustic music in this city, with big-name bluegrass players, jam sessions, and songwriters' showcases.

6051 Club, 6051 Forest Lane. Home of mainstream jazz for musicians and serious fans, located in a north Dallas shopping center.

DENVER

Ramada Renaissance Hotel, 3200 South Parker Road. Voted the best Denver piano bar. Features "Big Daddy Allen" and his piano.

My Brother's Bar, 2376 Fifteenth Street. An unpretentious, artsy bar on the bank of the South Platte River, where philosophical discussions are underscored by the sounds of Mozart. The owner brothers sponsor classical concerts in the park in the summer.

DETROIT

Archibald's, 555 South Woodward Avenue. Contemporary jazz.

FORT LAUDERDALE

Spyglass Lounge, Bahia Mar Hotel, 801 Seabreeze Boulevard. The piano player can shift from island music to Cole Porter.

FORT WORTH

J.R.'s Place, 3400 Bernie Anderson Road at Camp Bowie. A former pro football player, not TV's "Dallas" villain, owns the place. Fabulous jazz artists play nightly.

Pepper's, 3002 West 7th Street. Rhythm and blues, cool jazz, acoustic rock, and fusion jazz accompany the chili and burger fare.

HOUSTON

Rockefeller's, 3620 Washington. Varied entertainment, from local talent to nationally known artists; from folksy bluegrass to rock and jazz.

Birdwatchers, 907 Westheimer. Versatile vocal and piano trios in a crowded, stylized treehouse.

LOS ANGELES

Baked Potato, 3787 Cahuenga Boulevard, North Hollywood. Great local jazz acts nightly.

Concerts by the Sea, 100 Fisherman's Wharf, Redondo Beach. Two or three shows nightly in this elegant showcase.

Donte's, 4269 Lankershim Boulevard, North Hollywood. Mainline jazz greats.

The Golden Bear, 306 Pacific Coast Highway, Huntington Beach. Rock, jazz, et cetera for established acts and hopefuls.

Blues pianist

Simply Blues, 6290 Sunset Boulevard, Hollywood. Piano entertainment nightly; new talent showcase.

MIAMI

Konover Hotel, Empire Room, 5445 Collins Avenue. Visiting pianists such as Dave Brubeck and Ahmad Jamal.

Monty's Conch, 2560 South Bayshore Drive, Coconut Grove. Live music—calypso, rock, mellow jazz; piano bar.

MINNEAPOLIS/ST. PAUL

Night Train, 289 Como Avenue. A piano occupies the center of the room, under a skylight and next to two railroad cars locked together as part of the décor. Jazz, classical—the mood of the music varies.

NEW ORLEANS

Tipitina's, 501 Napoleon Avenue. The hippies who took over this place, establishing what is now a New Orleans institution, also brought back the once-great pianist Professor Longhair and made him a star again. Music offered here includes jazz, ska, reggae, rock 'n' roll, zydeco, and Caribbean Cajun, served up alongside Creole cooking. A funky hangout.

Pat O'Brien's, 718 St. Peter Street. Located in the city's French Quarter, O'Brien's has three bar areas, and keeps a staff of twelve pianists, who play two at a time.

NEW YORK

Algonquin, 59 West 44th Street. Pianist Steve Ross plays the songs of Noel Coward, and other witty tunes, in the urbane Oak Room of this legendary literary hotel.

Bradley's, 70 University Place at 11th Street. Some of the most accomplished famous pianists play in this dark-paneled, very talky New York bar and restaurant.

Michael's Pub, 211 East 55th Street. The ultimate supper club, with the finest musicians, among them George Shearing, Dick Hyman, and Marian McPartland. Even Woody Allen gets a kick out of playing his clarinet here.

Mikell's, 760 Columbus Avenue at 97th Street. For more than a decade, the rhythm-and-blues headquarters in New York. Famous neighborhood nightspot.

Village Vanguard, 178 Seventh Avenue S. at 11th Street. Just what people expect in a jazz club: crowded, smoky, with enthusiastic patrons and jazz musicians who knock your socks off. Photos of the piano greats who have played here line the walls. "Hot jazz here."

PHILADELPHIA

The Borgia Cafe, 408 South Second Street. Near Penn's Landing. Great live jazz every night, along with plenty of Society Hill gossip.

PORTLAND

Bogart's Joint, 406 N.W. 14th Street. Another "Casablanca"-inspired nightspot. The piano player is strong on boogie-woogie and 1930s and '40s songs. A unique spot loaded with Bogart memorabilia.

ST. LOUIS

Fox & Hounds Tavern, The Cheshire Inn, 6300 Clayton Road. The piano player stirs up this cozy old English tavern.

SAN DIEGO

Blue Parrot, 1298 Prospect Street, La Jolla. An elegant setting for top local jazzmen during the week, plus musicians from Los Angeles and New York on the weekends.

Crossroad Jazz, 345 Market Street, downtown. The best local jazz in San Diego's oldest jazz club, in the Gaslamp Quarter.

SAN FRANCISCO

Bach Dancing & Dynamite Society, Douglas Beach House, Miramar Beach, Half Moon Bay. Exciting live performers: blues, rock, and jazz at the water's edge, a spectacular setting for music.

Bajone's, 1062 Valencia Street. One of the hottest jazz joints in town, blending jazz, salsa, and rhythm and blues in the heart of the Mission District.

Henry Africa's, 2260 Van Ness. Everything's campy: the piano is suspended on a platform ten feet high, and the jazz/rock music makes the place jump.

Steve Ross at supper in the Algonquin Oak Room by Al Hirschfeld

No Name Bar, 757 Bridgeway Road, Sausalito. Live music alternates with jazz tapes and new wave in this woodsy, trendy, popular bar.

SEATTLE

Ray's Boathouse, 6049 Seaview Avenue NW. A subtle musical background for this chic, classy restaurant that has a spectacular view of Puget Sound and the Olympic Mountains.

Ernestine's, 313 Occidental South. Located in Pioneer Square, the oldest part of town. Features name jazz and pop/rock musicians.

WASHINGTON, D.C.

Charlie's Georgetown, 3223 K Street NW. Everyone, from political hotshots to students, comes to Charlie's. There's a small-scale nightclub with famous players, and also a piano bar crowded with people chumming and singing along at the piano.

Food for Thought, 1738 Connecticut Avenue NW. A neighborhood bar and natural food restaurant with jazz, folk and blues performers nightly.

F. Scott's, 1232 Thirty-Sixth Street NW. As the writer put it, this is for the rich and stylish. Music from the 1930s, '40s, and '50s.

King's Loft, 121 South Union Street, Alexandria. Piano bar jazz in the riverfront lounge.

A Guide to Discographies and Perennials

The amount of recorded piano music available today is so vast it could stymie even the most knowledgeable piano lover. Consequently, I have devised a guide to discographies, which lists the best record guides and catalogues in circulation, and also gives background information about performers, composers, and musical styles. The flip side to this guide is a selection of what I call "perennial recordings"—albums that are considered almost classic by general consensus: they are always either in stock or being reissued. They can serve as the gateway for what I hope will be your own future musical discoveries.

DISCOGRAPHIES

These will give you a good head start. Simply look up the name of the performer, the composer, or the composition to see what is available and what has been written about it.

The Schwann Catalogue. Record and Tape Guide (Schwann Record Catalogue, Boston). Practically an institution, this is *the* catalogue for classical music, but it also now covers pop, rock, jazz, country, et cetera. The *Schwann* is revised every month and is extremely accurate. It has listings, not recommendations—all twenty-eight listings, for example, of Beethoven's *Emperor* Piano Concerto. You can buy the *Schwann* for $1.50, or refer to it at most record stores. Besides the regular catalogue, *Schwann-1*, there's *Schwann-2* for older, "mono" records.

The 101 Best Jazz Albums: A History of Jazz on Records, by Len Lyons (Morrow/Quill, New York, 1980). A comprehensive listener's guide to ragtime, New Orleans, swing, bebop, modern fusion, and free jazz. An excellent introduction to jazz, with biographies and a multitude of selected albums.

The Rolling Stone Record Guide, edited by Dave Marsh with John Swenson (Random House/Rolling Stone Press Book, New York, 1979). Reviews and ratings of almost ten thousand currently available rock, pop, soul, country, blues, jazz, and gospel albums. Although it's now a few years old, this is still the best rock guide around.

The New Penguin Stereo Record & Cassette Guide, by Edward Greenfield, Robert Layton, and Ivan March (Penguin Books, Middlesex, England, 1982). Commentary and record recommendations as well as listings. A comprehensive guide.

The Illustrated Encyclopedia of Jazz, by Brian Case and Stan Britt (Harmony Books, New York, 1978). A comprehensive, colorful, "A to Z" volume giving a discography within the context of the pianist-composer's musical evolution. From Scott Joplin to Cecil Taylor and beyond.

The Illustrated Encyclopedia of Classical Music, by Lionel Salter (Harmony Books, New York, 1978). A guide to composers and recommended recordings. European oriented, since the series was first published in England. A useful, attractive way to know the composer's lifetime output.

The Illustrated Encyclopedia of Rock, compiled by Nick Logan and Bob Woffinden. New edition. (Harmony Books, New York, 1978.) The third volume in this series, this guide gives a discography for keyboardists and groups (and shows record covers).

Magazines from the various musical domains do reviews of most of the new albums. You'll find regular critiques in: *Stereo Review* (for classical music); *Gramophone* (also for classical, an English publication); *Keynote* (classical, a radio station's magazine); *Keyboard* (all domains); *Ovation* (classical); *Downbeat* and *Crawdaddy* (jazz and pop); *Rolling Stone* (rock and pop). There are many other publications—both magazines and newspapers—that regularly review new records, from *Playboy* to the *Los Angeles Times.*

CLASSICAL PERENNIALS

Bach (Johann Sebastian). Rosalyn Tureck is a well-established Bach interpreter—listen to her "Italian Concerto" or "Chromatic Fantasy and Fugue." So is Glenn Gould; especially good are his "Goldberg Variations," which he rerecorded on digital just before his death, and his "Well-Tempered Clavier" and "Art of the Fugue." People either love or hate Gould's records because of his always original, if unorthodox, interpretations, but he's definitely to be reckoned with. Arturo Benedetti Michaelangeli

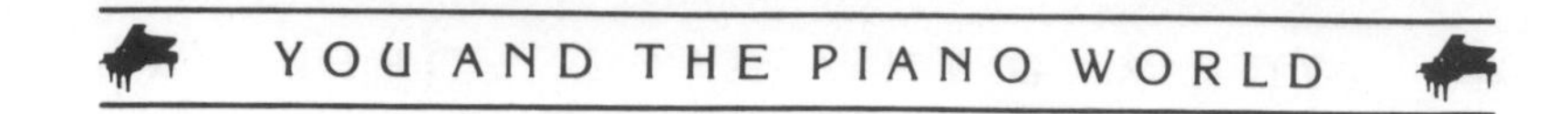

is known for his Bach; pieces to listen to might include the Partitas and the Bach-Busoni Chaconne. If you prefer Bach played on the harpsichord, as it was written, try Wanda Landowska's definitive recordings.

Barber, Samuel. "Piano Sonata," recorded by John Browning or Ruth Laredo, is recommended.

Bartók. Any recordings by the Rumanian pianist Dinu Lipatti or the Hungarian Gyorgy Sandor.

Beethoven. Quite a few pianists are known for their Beethoven, particularly Artur Schnabel, Rudolf Serkin, Claudio Arrau, Wilhelm Kempff, Daniel Barenboim, and Vladimir Ashkenazy. Some have recorded all thirty-two sonatas (including the monstrous "Hammerklavier"), and all five piano concerti, as well as chamber music (piano trios, et cetera). Smaller pieces include the "Diabelli Variations."

Brahms. Backhaus was one of the ultimate Brahms pianists, and his records are generally available. Rubinstein is superlative for Brahms. Alfred Brendel is good (for the two concerti), as is Arturo Benedetti Michaelangeli, and Vladimir Ashkenazy, particularly for the First Piano Concerto, as conducted by Bernard Haitink with the Concertgebouw Philharmonic. Brahms piano pieces include rhapsodies, ballades, et cetera.

PIANO HIT PARADE

The first classical record to sell a million copies was of a performance of Tchaikovsky's *Piano Concerto No. 1* that featured pianist Van Cliburn. This recording was made in 1958, after Cliburn had created a worldwide sensation by being the first American pianist to win the Tchaikovsky Competition in Moscow. Record sales reached 1 million by 1961, 2 million by 1965, and about 2,500,000 by January 1970.

- **The greatest-selling classical record of all time is *Switched-on Bach* by Walter Carlos. It features many of Bach's best-known works, realized entirely on a Moog synthesizer.**
- **Artur Rubinstein was the best-selling classical pianist in history. He made more than 200 records, which sold 10 million copies.**

Carter, Elliott. Twentieth-century piano music. Try Carter's "Piano Sonata" and "Night Fantasies" played by Paul Jacobs (Nonesuch).

Chopin. Rubinstein, of course, is wonderful for Chopin. Horowitz is another par excellence interpreter of Chopin, although very different from Rubinstein. You're also safe with Maurizio Pollini, André Watts, Arturo Benedetti Michaelangeli, Vladimir Ashkenazy, Guiomar Novaes (an excellent Brazilian pianist) and Dinu Lipatti. Chopin piano music includes ballades, polonaises, études, preludes, scherzos, impromptus, waltzes, and mazurkas.

Copland. "Four Piano Blues," performed by Paul Jacobs and William Bolcom, is particularly recommended, along with other piano works.

Crumb, George. *Makrokosmos*—either volume 1 (David Burge) or 2 (Robert Miller) for more modern music.

Debussy. Walter Gieseking (also for other impressionist composers). French pianists such as Robert Casadesus, Alfred Cortot, and Philippe Entremont. Other greats for Debussy: Rubinstein, Claudio Arrau, Guiomar Novaes. Debussy wrote

twenty-four preludes, the *Children's Corner* suite, "Images," "Estampes," "Etudes," and many other piano works.

Granados. Alicia de Larrocha gives definitive performances. Listen to her "Goyescas" or "Danzas Españolas." (It's also de Larrocha, along with Rubinstein, for the other great Spanish composers—particularly good is de Larrocha's recording of "Iberia," by Albeniz.)

Grieg. Emil Gilels and Rubinstein. There's only one Grieg concerto, but many lyrical and other piano pieces.

Liszt. Quite a few pianists are marvelous for Liszt: Vladimir Horowitz, of course, and also Lazar Berman, André Watts, Daniel Barenboim, and Sviatoslav Richter. These pianists play Liszt's "killer pieces"—some of the most difficult piano music ever written: the "Mephisto Waltz," "Consolations," "Transcendental Etudes," Années de Pèlerinage" (Years of Pilgrimage), the Sonata in B-minor, as well as the Hungarian Rhapsodies and the Paganini Etudes.

Mozart. Recordings by Geza Anda, Murray Perahia, Alfred Brendel, Walter Gieseking, Radu Lupu, and Christoph Eschenbach. Twenty-seven piano concerti, seventeen sonatas, and much other great music.

Prokofiev. Sonatas recorded by Gilels or Richter.

Rachmaninoff. It's Horowitz for Rachmaninoff—and for all the other Russian composers. Also excellent are Van Cliburn, Ruth Laredo, and Lazar Berman. Four concerti, sonatas, "Rhapsody on a Theme by Paganini," et cetera.

Ravel. Again, it's Walter Gieseking for the impressionists; also Philippe Entremont. Piano pieces from "Miroirs" and "Pavane for a Dead Princess" to the four-hand "Mother Goose Suite" and the blockbuster "Gaspard de la Nuit."

Rzewski, Frederic. "The People Will Never Be Defeated," performed by Ursula Oppens. An avant-garde composer who is distinctive.

Scarlatti, Domenico. Keyboard sonatas played by Horowitz and de Larrocha.

Schubert. André Watts, Emil Gilels, Radu Lupu, Alfred Brendel, and Vladimir Ashkenazy. The "Wanderer Fantasy," Sonatas in A-Minor and in A-Major, the "Impromptu."

Schumann. The all-time greats for Schumann are Rubinstein, Horowitz, and Novaes. Well-known Schumann works available on fine recordings include "Fantasiestücke," "Carnival," "Fantasy in C," "Kreisleriana," and "Davidsbündlertänze."

Scriabin. Vladimir Horowitz, Ruth Laredo, and Lazar Berman. Sonatas, études, and other piano pieces.

Tchaikovsky. All the greats: Sviatoslav Richter, Vladimir Horowitz, Artur Rubinstein, Emil Gilels. The piano concertos are especially recommended; also try the new recording by Martha Argerich of the No. 1 concerto, with Kiril Kondrashin conducting the Bavarian Radio Symphony.

And of course you'll never go wrong with the complete recorded works of Artur Rubinstein or Vladimir Horowitz!

Keith Jarrett

JAZZ PERENNIALS

Eubie Blake. Albums such as: *The 86 Years of Eubie Blake* (two-record set, Columbia Records)—includes songs such as "Tricky Fingers" and "Troublesome Ivories"; *The Wizard of the Ragtime Piano* (20th Century Fox); *Wild About Eubie* (Warner Bros. Records).

The Dave Brubeck Quartet. *Dave Brubeck's All-Time Greatest Hits* (Columbia Records), with the classic "Take Five."

Claude Bolling. Jazzy "crossover" albums with classical artists. *Suite for Flute and Jazz Piano* features Jean-Pierre Rampal; *Suite for Violin and Jazz Piano* features Pinchas Zukerman (Columbia/CBS).

Ray Charles. *The Great Ray Charles* (Atlantic)—Ray Charles at the piano, with band arrangements by Quincy Jones.

Chick Corea. On Miles Davis's historic album, *Bitches Brew* (Columbia/CBS); and with his old group, Return to Forever, on their album *Romantic Warrior.*

Duke Ellington. Where to start with one of the greatest, most prolific jazz composers and arrangers? With *Duke Ellington—1940* (Smithsonian Collection), for songs such as "Body and Soul"; *The Golden Duke* (two-record set, Prestige), which includes "Take the 'A' Train"; *Pure Gold* (RCA) for "Black and Tan Fantasy."

Bill Evans. To begin with, *Village Vanguard Sessions* (Milestone).

George Gershwin. André Watts playing the solo version of "Rhapsody in Blue," plus preludes and songs, on *By Watts* (Columbia); Peter Nero's orchestral version of the "Rhapsody," with Arthur Fiedler and the Boston Pops; André Previn playing both the "Rhapsody" and "An American in Paris" with the London Symphony Orchestra (Angel).

Herbie Hancock. The historic *Headhunters* (Columbia/CBS), with its rhythmic riffs; *V.S.O.P.: The Quintet* (two-record set, Columbia), a reunion album with Wayne Shorter, Freddie Hubbard, and others.

Keith Jarrett. *The Köln Concert* (two-record set, ECM) especially, but *all* of his albums are intriguing.

Scott Joplin. *Piano Rags*, volumes I, II, and III, played by Joshua Rifkin (Nonesuch); Dick Hyman's *Scott Joplin: The Complete Works for Piano* (RCA).

Marian McPartland. *From This Moment On* (Concord); *Live at the Carlyle* (Halcyon).

Modern Jazz Quartet. John Lewis is the well-known pianist here. *Modern Jazz Quartet* (Atlantic), an album with songs such as "Django" and "It Don't Mean a Thing (If It Ain't Got That Swing)."

Thelonious Monk. *Genius of Modern Music*, with Art Blakey and Milt Jackson (Blue Note); *The Complete Genius* (Blue Note), which includes "Round Midnight" and "Ruby, My Dear."

Peter Nero. His first album, *New Piano in Town* (Applause); *Peter Goes Pop* (Applause), with show tunes such as "Send in the Clowns" and "The Wiz."

Oscar Peterson. *In Concert* (two-record set, Verve) includes "Falling in Love with Love," "Gypsy in My Soul"; *History of an Artist* (Pablo).

Art Tatum. There's no way to go wrong with Tatum. Try *Art Tatum: Masterpieces (1941–1944)* (MCA), which includes his famous "Tiger Rag," his reunion with past sidemen; *Solo Piano* (Capitol); *The Tatum Solo Masterpieces* (Pablo), Volumes 1–9 (separately or in a boxed set), recorded near the end of his extraordinary career.

Billy Taylor. *Jazz Alive* (Monmouth Evergreen).

Fats Waller. *Fats Waller Piano Solos,* 1929–1941 (two-record set, Bluebird), with "Handful of Keys"; the Broadway musical, *Ain't Misbehavin',* 1978, original cast (two-record set, RCA).

Mary Lou Williams. *I Love a Piano* (Esquire); "From the Heart," solo (Chiaroscuro).

ROCK, POPULAR, AND OTHER PERENNIALS

Featuring the acoustic piano are:

The Blasters. Live album with Gene Taylor on piano (Slash Records).

Blondie. Parallel Lines (Chrysalis), with Jimmy Destri on keyboards.

Elvis Costello and the Attractions. Imperial Bedroom (Columbia/CBS); keyboardist is Steve Nieve.

Fleetwood Mac. Christine McVie is quite a piano player. Albums such as *Fleetwood Mac* and *Rumours* (both from Warner Bros.).

Joe Jackson. On *Night and Day* (A&M Records), Jackson spins loose on the ivories.

Billy Joel. All of Joel's records are piano oriented. You might choose *Piano Man* or *Nylon Curtain* (both from Columbia).

Elton John. Also piano oriented. Particularly strong on piano are the albums *Tumbleweed Connection, Honky Chateau, Goodbye Yellow Brick Road,* and *Don't Shoot Me, I'm Only the Piano Player* (all from MCA).

Carole King. A strong pianist. A classic album is *Tapestry* (Ode).

Randy Newman. Talented, eccentric performer-composer, an excellent pianist; albums such as *Sail Away* (Reprise) and *Trouble in Paradise* (Warner Bros.).

Hammond organ:

Keith Emerson. Emerson is a rock keyboard virtuoso: piano, organ, synthesizers, et cetera. With his group, the Nice, he made such albums as *Elegy* (Mercury/Charisma), with amazing organ solos. With Emerson, Lake and Palmer, his major group, he made *Brain Salad Surgery* (Manticore).

Electric and electronic pianos:

Supertramp. Dreamer and *Breakfast in America* (both from A&M); British group with very good keyboards and other instrumentals.

Stevie Wonder. Talking Book, which includes the song "Superstition"; *Innervisions,* with "Higher Ground" (Tamla); many other excellent albums.

Synthesizers:

Walter Carlos. Switched on Bach (Columbia)—Bach gone electronic for the first time.

Chariots of Fire, by Vangelis (Polydor). Award-winning musical score, lush synthesizer sound, from the movie.

Peter Gabriel. Peter Gabriel (Atco/Charisma), with Larry Fast on synthesizers.

Jan Hammer. Birds of Fire (Columbia/CBS), the Mahavishnu Orchestra.

Kraftwerk. An innovative German group that has played amazingly with synthesizers; *Autobahn* (Vertigo) will give you some idea of what they're about.

Isao Tomita. This Japanese composer has done a synthesized version of Debussy's music in *Snowflakes Are Dancing* (RCA); he has also updated other classical composers with originality.

Rick Wakeman. A dropout from England's Royal College of Music, Wakeman has gone for grand concept and production themes, with albums such as *The Six Wives of Henry VIII* and the soundtrack for Lisztomania (A&M).

Weather Report. Hard to classify—perhaps "jazz/rock fusion" is the best category. Joe Zawinul is the sensational Austrian keyboardist and composer. Albums such as *Weather Report, I Sing the Body Electric,* and *Heavy Weather* (all from Columbia/CBS).

THE PIANO

The piano sits Grand
Thick and
Curled
Stringed and Keyed
on three legs

It emanates the Dreams it was
given

Made of raw energy
more or less squeezed into
the shape of a potential
Messenger of the Secret of Life Itself
Its maker asks it to be
further imbued

It sometimes feels like a magnet
Whose pull would
push its taker
through the other side of
the thinnest of ridges
which separates
flesh from spirit
from Sound to Song
from Body to Beauty
from Rhythm to Infinity
from Notes to Music

From *Music Poetry* by Chick Corea

Glossary

acoustic. **Has to do with hearing or with sound as it is heard. But with regard to the piano, refers to the instrument whose sound is produced "naturally," without electric or electronic devices.**

action (piano). **The mechanism that transmits the action of the fingers to the sound-producing parts; in keyboard instruments, the action forms the essential, characteristic part of the instrument. A piano action, for example, is the instrument's most complicated mechanism.**

arpeggio (Italian). **A broken chord; that is, a chord whose notes are performed one after another instead of together, usually beginning with the lowest note and ending with the highest.**

clavier. **Generic designation for the stringed keyboard instruments, especially the clavichord, harpsichord, and pianoforte.**

concerto (Italian). **A composition for orchestra and a solo instrument, usually a piano or violin. Generally the parts of the soloist and orchestra are about equal in importance. Most concertos (or concerti) have three movements. The first movement is usually in sonata form and often includes a cadenza (in which the soloist demonstrates his virtuosity) near the end. The second movement is generally in slow tempo, and the third is most often a lively rondo, or in the form of a theme with variations or in sonata form.**

étude (the French word for study). **An instrumental piece designed to improve the player's technique. Etudes usually contain technically difficult material—arpeggios, trills, octaves, et cetera. Although some études are principally technical studies, others may contain material that is beautiful from a musical standpoint—for example, Chopin's piano études.**

harmony. **The pattern of intervals and chords in a musical composition. Also, the study of chords and intervals, of the ways in which chords and intervals are related to one another, and the ways in which one interval or chord can be connected together.**

improvisation. **The invention of music—a whole composition, a variation on a theme, or ornamentation of a repeated section—at the same time that it is being performed. In earlier periods the ability to improvise was considered essential for most musicians. Mozart, Beethoven, Mendelssohn, and Liszt, for example, were extraordinary improvisers. Today it is an important element of jazz, and often used in jazz/rock.**

melody. **A group of musical tones sounded one after another, together making up a meaningful whole. The total melody makes** sense to the ear, and can usually be remembered, at least in part. In the most general sense, it is a succession of musical tones, as contrasted with harmony—that is, musical tones sounded simultaneously. Thus, melody and harmony represent the horizontal and the vertical elements of the musical texture; rhythm is considered to be the third basic musical element.

octave. All eight tones of any major or minor scale. Also, the interval between the first and eighth tones (in rising order of pitch) in a major or minor scale. The eighth tone of the diatonic scale is also called the octave. The octave is the most perfect consonance, so perfect that it gives the impression of being a mere duplication of the original tone.

perfect (or absolute) pitch. The ability to identify a musical tone by name, or to sing a particular tone, without the help of first hearing some other tone. Perfect pitch is thought by many, but not all, musical experts to be an inborn ability.

piano. A stringed keyboard instrument. The keys cause hammers to strike the strings by means of a connecting mechanism called the action. This causes the strings to sound. Scientifically, as a sound-producing agent, the piano is classified as a stringed instrument, the strings of which are stretched over a board—the sounding board. *Piano* is also an abbreviation of the instrument's original name, *pianoforte,* Italian for "soft-loud," which refers to the fact that the player can produce softer or louder tones by varying his touch (finger pressure) on the keys.

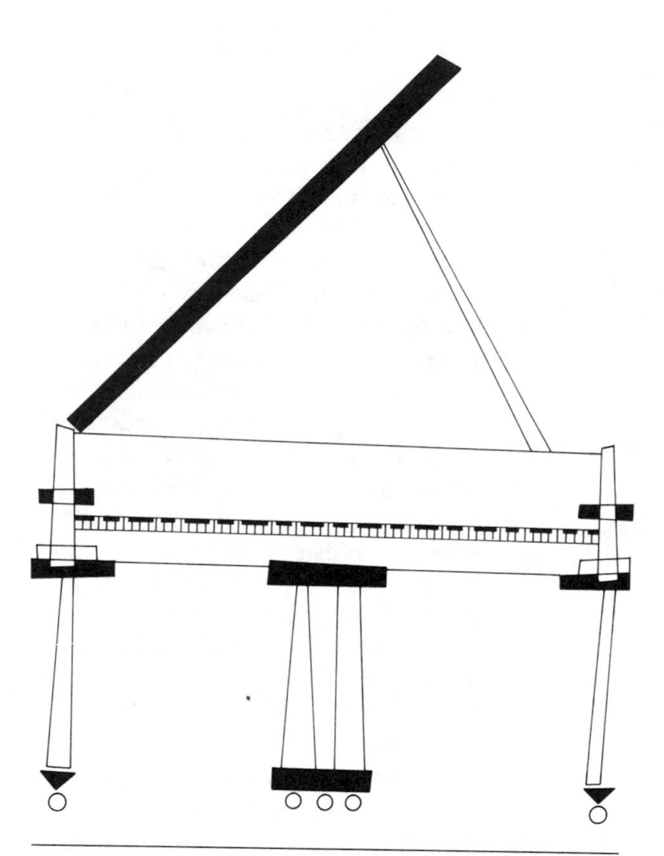

Piano, designed by Randall De Leeuw

pitch. The location of a musical sound in the tonal scale, proceeding from low to high. Also, the highness or lowness of a musical tone. The pitch of a tone depends on its frequency: the number of vibrations per second of the string, air column, or other sound-producing agent.

rhythm. Everything pertaining to the temporal quality (duration) of the musical sound. How fast musical tones move (tempo) and what patterns are formed of long and short notes, as well as accents.

scale. A selection of tones within one octave, arranged in rising order of pitches. In Western (European and American) music these notes are a selection from the twelve halftones that make up an octave.

solfeggio. A kind of musical training, involving both ear training and sight-singing (the ability to sing a musical passage at sight). It involves learning to recognize clefs, key signatures, intervals, and rhythm—all the elements of musical notation—and to translate them into actual sounds.

sonata. A composition for piano or other instrument that consists of three or four independent pieces, called movements, each of which follows certain standards of character and form. Practically all the features of the sonata are also found in certain other types of instrumental music—the symphony, certain chamber music (quartets, trios), and, with certain modifications, the concerto. The normal scheme for the movements of a sonata is: Allegro, Adagio, Scherzo (or Minuet), Allegro. This scheme is observed in the great majority of sonatas. One exception is Beethoven's *Moonlight Sonata,* which consists of Adagio, Scherzo, Presto.

virtuoso. A highly skilled musical performer, particularly with regard to technical ability. The term also describes a musical composition that requires great technical skill.

Treble/Bass Clef,
designed by Randall De Leeuw

Recommended Reading

PIANISTS

Conversations with Arrau by Joseph Horowitz. New York: Alfred A. Knopf, 1983. Claudio Arrau, at eighty, talks about his life and his music, providing an insight into the workings of great pianism.

The Great Pianists from Mozart to the Present, by Harold C. Schonberg. New York: Fireside-Simon and Schuster, 1963. Piano performance since its inception 200 years ago, from Mozart to Van Cliburn, by the former music critic for the *New York Times.*

Horowitz: A Biography, by Glenn Plaskin. New York: William C. Morrow & Co., 1983. Horowitz's first biographer gives a musical analysis of his playing and a behind-the-scenes portrait of his legendary career.

I Really Should Be Practicing, by Gary Graffman. New York: Doubleday, 1981. A well-known concert pianist shares his memories of musical giants such as Toscanini and Rachmaninoff, friendships with pianists such as Horowitz, and thirty years of concert tours from Baden-Baden to Bora-Bora.

My Young Years, by Artur Rubinstein. New York: Alfred A. Knopf, 1973. Volume one of his two-volume autobiography. A born storyteller, Rubinstein recounts his gloriously misspent youth, his early musical experiences, and his friendships with the artistic giants of the century. Volume one takes him from his birth in 1887 to World War I.

My Many Years, by Artur Rubinstein. New York: Alfred A. Knopf, 1980. The second volume continues with his musical conquest of South America, other memorable concert tours, and the exciting artistic circle in Paris of which he was the center.

PIANO HISTORY AND MANUFACTURING

Giraffes, Black Dragons, and Other Pianos, by Edwin M. Good. Stanford: Stanford University Press, 1983. A chronicle outlining the piano's evolution.

Men, Women and Pianos: A Social History, by Arthur Loesser. New York: Simon and Schuster, 1954. A social, political, economic, and technological history of the piano that has become a classic. Chapters include "Pianos Become a Business," "Beethoveniana Pianistica," and "The Keyboards Go West."

The Piano: Its Story, from Zither to Grand, by David S. Grover. New York: Charles Scribner's Sons, 1978. A piano manufacturer discusses the piano's technical development.

"The Quality of the Instrument: Building Steinway Grand Piano K 2571," by Michael Lenehan. Boston: *Atlantic Monthly*, August 1982. (Back copies available through the *Atlantic Monthly*; reprints from Steinway & Sons, New York.) Lenehan documents the painstaking, yearlong process of making one Steinway grand piano, from choosing the lumber to the first performances on the brand new instrument.

The Book of the Piano, edited by Dominic Gill. Ithaca: Cornell University Press, 1981. A comprehensive study of the piano, written by fourteen distinguished musicologists and performing musicians.

Lives of the Piano, edited by James R. Gaines. New York: Holt, Rinehart & Winston, 1980. Essays on various aspects of the piano by writers and musicians, including Anthony Burgess, Ned Rorem, and William Bolcom.

The Piano Makers, written and photographed by David Anderson. New York: Pantheon Books, 1982. An illustrated look at how a piano is actually made, through a tour of the Steinway factory. Written for children, but also informative for adults.

PIANO PURCHASE, CARE, AND PLAYING

The Jamey Aebersold Series (book and record sets). New York: Aebersold, 1982. For those who want to learn or improve their jazz improvisation. Albums feature recordings by jazz musicians such as Duke Ellington and Horace Silver, playing piano, bass, and drums. You play along, learning tunes by ear and by the book.

Pierce Piano Atlas, eighth edition, by Bob Pierce. Long Beach, CA: Pierce Publications, 1982. A directory of extensive listings (116,000) of pianos by name of company, name, date of manufacture, and serial number. If you're shopping for a piano or want to discover its date of manufacture, this is very useful for identifying a piano's age and natal origins.

The Piano Owner's Guide: How to Buy and Care for a Piano (revised edition) by Carl D. Schmeckel. New York: Charles Scribner's, 1974. Practical advice on the care, feeding, maintenance, tuning, moving, cleaning, and repairing of a piano. Everything from advice on how to eliminate "that pesky mouse" that may make a home in your piano to a discussion of how grand and upright pianos actually work.

With Your Own Two Hands: Self-Discovery through Music by Seymour Bernstein. New York: Schirmer Books, 1981. A noted teacher gives step-by-step guidelines for conquering various musical and technical problems at the piano. Bernstein uses new techniques, including biofeedback and choreographic movements, to demonstrate his points. He stimulates the reader to approach practicing and piano playing from an entirely new standpoint, and brings a humanistic approach to both.

GENERAL MUSIC LORE

Harvard Dictionary of Music, by Willi Apel. Cambridge, MA: Harvard University Press, 1979. Revised, enlarged edition. A musical dictionary for both musical amateurs and scholars. Provides musical history and technical definitions. (Far more complete is the *New Grove Dictionary of Music and Musicians* for $1,900.)

The Joy of Music, by Leonard Bernstein. New York: Fireside-Simon and Schuster, 1959. An "adventure in musical understanding" by one of America's favorite composers, conductors, interpreters, and pianists.

The Encyclopedia of Jazz in the Seventies, by Leonard Feather. New York: Horizon Press, 1976. A complete survey of the genre, with 2000 biographies and 200 photographs. By one of America's best-known jazz historians and critics.

Rock Hardware, edited by Tony Bacon. New York: Harmony Books, 1981 (originally published by Quill Publishing, London). Filled with information, graphics, and an up-to-date section on electronic and acoustic pianos, synthesizers, and the people who play them, including Elton John, Keith Emerson, and Isao Tomita.

What to Listen for in Music, by Aaron Copland. New York: New American Library, 1956. Composer Aaron Copland offers suggestions for listening to all genres of music from a composer's point of view.

PIANO MAGAZINES

Keyboard Magazine (monthly). Its "ecumenical" musical scope covers jazz, rock, classical, country, popular, and blues, and features pianists and keyboardists. Their advisory board includes Dave Brubeck, André Watts, and Oscar Peterson.

Ovation (monthly). Classical only. Features pianists such as Claudio Arrau, Vladimir Ashkenazy, Vladimir Horowitz. Includes interviews, record reviews, developments in music, and a "Pianists to Keep an Eye On" column. A "Keys to the Keyboard" column is devoted to "piano purchase, care, and repertoire."

Clavier (monthly). Classical only. Board of directors includes Alicia de Larrocha, Leon Fleisher, and Beveridge Webster. Emphasis on piano teaching.

Keyboard Classics (bimonthly). Calls itself "the magazine you can play." One-third of issue consists of piano pieces by composers such as Mozart, Clementi, and Rachmaninoff. Discusses music history, technique, musicianship, and records.

Downbeat (monthly). Jazz oriented. Informative columns, reviews, features, and interviews with jazz pianists.

Rolling Stone, *Musician*, and *Trouser Press*. These publications occasionally print pieces on pianists or keyboardists, and offer record and concert reviews and up-to-date news on musicians, instruments, and technology.

About the Author

Judith Oringer has published numerous interviews with artists and writes about music, literature, politics, and women. She has been an editor for the Playboy Book Club, writer for *Ramparts,* and a reader for the Book-of-the-Month Club, Warner Bros., and Orion Films. She is currently a French interpreter for the U.S. State Department and resides in New York City.

Contents: Artur Rubinstein courtesy RCA records; Spinetto courtesy Metropolitan Museum of Art, Joseph Pulitzer Bequest, 1953; Museum of Modern Art Film Stills Archives; Leonard Bernstein courtesy CBS Records. Page xiii: © 1982 John de Amicus. Page xiv: All photos © Lawrence Frank. Page xvi: Library of Congress. Page 2: Both photos courtesy Smithsonian. Page 3: Chamber organ and clavichord courtesy Metropolitan Museum of Art, Crosby Brown Collection of Musical Instruments, 1889. Page 6: Top six photos courtesy Metropolitan Museum of Art; Bottom three courtesy Moravian Historical Society, Library of Congress, New York Public Library Picture Collection. Page 7: Gene Bagnato. Page 8: Left, courtesy Metropolitan Museum of Art, Crosby Brown Collection. Page 9: Courtesy Metropolitan Museum of Art, Gift of Mrs. Henry McSweeney, 1959. Page 10: Two left photos courtesy Smithsonian. Page 11: © Ebet Roberts. Page 14: Gribbet. Page 15: Steve Satterwhite. Page 16: Courtesy CBS-Don Hunstein. Page 18: Deborah Feingold. Page 19: Sotheby Parke Bernet. Page 20: Library of Congress. Page 21: Right, Kristin Murphy. Page 22: Both photos Wide World. Page 23: UPI; Steinway. Page 24: Kristin Murphy. Page 25: Steinway; Photo of Henry Steinway by Matthew Brady. Page 30: Wide World. Page 31: Tony King; Kalman Detrich. Page 32: Thomas Hahn. Page 33: Thomas Hahn; Metropolitan Museum of Art, Crosby Brown Collection; Thomas Hahn. Page 35: Library of Congress. Page 37: Cartoon by Gerard Hoffnung; model piano George Denninger, Pool courtesy of Liberace. Page 39: New York Public Library. Page 40: Thomas Hahn. Page 41: New York Public Library. Page 42: Library of Congress. Page 44: Courtesy Museum of Modern Art, New York, Philip L. Goodwin Collection. Page 46: Stockholm National Museum. Page 47: Steinway. Page 48: Piano and crane, Wide World; Piano and helicopter, Steinway. Page 49: Lawrence Frank. Page 51: Barnes Foundation. Page 52: Culver Pictures. Page 53: Bösendorfer. Page 54: Betty Lee Hunt Associates, Columbia Artists Management, copyright by Francesco Scavullo. Page 55: John Russell. Page 56: Bob James by Arlene Kriv. Page 59: Clara Schumann courtesy Culver Pictures; Jerry Lee Lewis courtesy of UPI. Page 61: CUNY. Page 62: Vladimir Horowitz copyright 1983 by Marianne Barcellona. Page 64: Library of Congress. Page 65: Kristen Murphy. Page 66: Library of Congress. Page 67: Acme Agency. Page 68: Library of Congress. Page 69: Elton John courtesy UPI; Liberace courtesy C. Zumwalt, photographer; Horowitz courtesy Wide World. Page 70: Betty Lee Hunt Associates. Page 71: Van Gogh painting courtesy Kuntsmuseum Basel. Page 72: Deborah Feingold. Page 75: Marianne Barcellona. Page 76: Copyright Norman Hecker. Page 77: Courtesy Alix Williamson. Page 78: Gershwin courtesy UPI; Lorin Hollander by Lawrence Frank. Page 79: Right, Federico Diaz. Page 80: Library of Congress. Page 81: Courtesy *New York Times*. Pages 83 and 84: Copyright Lawrence Frank. Page 85: Kodak. Page 86: SUNY. Page 87: Copyright © 1983 by Marianne Barcellona. Page 89: Courtesy Metropolitan Museum of Art, Robert Lehman Collection, 1975. Page 90: Copyright Dan Budnik, 1980. Page 91: Monkmeyer. Page 92: Left, Wide World; Right, Library of Congress. Page 93: UPI. Page 94: Library of Congress. Pages 95 and 96: © Lawrence Frank. Page 97: Library of Congress. Page 98: Copyright © Marianne Barcellona. Page 99: © Henry Grossman. Page 100: Copyright © Marianne Barcellona. Page 101: Steinway. Page 102: Baldwin. Page 103: C. Steiner. Page 104: Courtesy Columbia Pictures. Page 106: Library of Congress. Page 107: © Affiliated Artists. Page 108: Culver Pictures. Page 110: New York Public Library. Page 111: Library of Congress. Page 112: Steinway. Page 113: Willie Turey. Page 114: New York Public Library. Pages 116-117: All photos courtesy Museum of Modern Art/Film Stills Archive. Page 118: Left, Library of Congress; Right, Culver Pictures. Page 119: Library of Congress. Page 120: German Information Center. Page 121: Steinway. Page 122: Library of Congress. Page 127: Dog by Kurt Nurock; Cat by Michael Jacobi; Rabbit copyright 1980 by Micoud Designs Ltd. Page 128: Library of Congress. Page 130: Courtesy Library of Congress. Page 132: © Lawrence Frank. Page 138: Telefunken. Page 139: Norton and Peel. Page 141: Newport and KOOL jazz festivals by Federico Diaz. Page 143: Clockwise from top; E. List, Library of Congress, Ted Thai. Page 144: © Lawrence Frank. Page 146: Poster by Milton Glaser, courtesy Carnegie Hall. Page 150: National Archives. Page 155: Courtesy RCA. Page 157: Takashi Itoh. Page 162: © 1975 by the Toy Press. Page 163: Copyright 1982/Lake End Graphics. Alfred A. Knopf, *My Many Years,* by Artur Rubinstein. Piano logo by Katie Smith.